SpringerBriefs in Applied Sciences and Technology

SpringerBriefs present concise summaries of cutting-edge research and practical applications across a wide spectrum of fields. Featuring compact volumes of 50 to 125 pages, the series covers a range of content from professional to academic.

Typical publications can be:

- A timely report of state-of-the art methods
- An introduction to or a manual for the application of mathematical or computer techniques
- A bridge between new research results, as published in journal articles
- A snapshot of a hot or emerging topic
- An in-depth case study
- A presentation of core concepts that students must understand in order to make independent contributions

SpringerBriefs are characterized by fast, global electronic dissemination, standard publishing contracts, standardized manuscript preparation and formatting guidelines, and expedited production schedules.

On the one hand, **SpringerBriefs in Applied Sciences and Technology** are devoted to the publication of fundamentals and applications within the different classical engineering disciplines as well as in interdisciplinary fields that recently emerged between these areas. On the other hand, as the boundary separating fundamental research and applied technology is more and more dissolving, this series is particularly open to trans-disciplinary topics between fundamental science and engineering.

Indexed by EI-Compendex, SCOPUS and Springerlink.

More information about this series at http://www.springer.com/series/8884

Marcus M. Dapp · Dirk Helbing · Stefan Klauser
Editors

Finance 4.0—Towards a Socio-Ecological Finance System

A Participatory Framework to Promote Sustainability

 Springer

Editors
Marcus M. Dapp
Computational Social Science
ETH Zürich
Zürich, Switzerland

Dirk Helbing
Computational Social Science
ETH Zürich
Zürich, Switzerland

Stefan Klauser
Computational Social Science
ETH Zürich
Zürich, Switzerland

The editors acknowledge funding by the Swiss National Foundation for EU FLAG-ERA project "FuturICT 2.0—Large scale experiments and simulations for the second generation of FuturICT" under grant number 170226 (for more information see https://futurict2.eu).

ISSN 2191-530X   ISSN 2191-5318   (electronic)
SpringerBriefs in Applied Sciences and Technology
ISBN 978-3-030-71399-7   ISBN 978-3-030-71400-0   (eBook)
https://doi.org/10.1007/978-3-030-71400-0

This Springer imprint is published by the registered company Springer Nature Switzerland AG
The registered company address is: Gewerbestrasse 11, 6330 Cham, Switzerland

Preface

Ten years ago, in 2011, the FuturICT project was selected as the No. 1 European flagship pilot in the area of future and emerging technologies. Its goal was to understand and manage complex, global and socially interactive systems, focusing on sustainability and resilience.

By integrating Information and Communication Technology (ICT), complexity science and social sciences, it intended to promote a paradigm shift towards a symbiotic co-evolution of ICT and society. Leveraging data from complex, global ICT systems would enable the development of models of techno-socio-economic systems. In turn, insights from these models would shape a new generation of socially adaptive, self-organized ICT systems.

Following on from these flagship pilots, FLAG-ERA issued transnational calls to build communities kick-starting disruptive, new, large-scale research in Europe. The FuturICT 2.0 project was submitted and accepted for funding, starting in February 2017 for a four-year period.

At the heart of FuturICT 2.0, our team at the ETH Zürich node started to work on the idea for a socio-ecological finance system, Finance 4.0 (FIN4), which could advance sustainable societies through a bottom-up and self-organizing approach. Our goals were highly ambitious—creating a FIN4 community, building a demonstrator using emergent technologies and combining research with development. We, therefore, had to be resourceful, planning communication, events and coding cycles in a way that allowed us to get the most out of these years. Furthermore, we wanted to involve bachelor, master and doctoral students.

Together with our partners, we organized the BIOTS Blockchain and Internet of Things (IoT) School, later becoming the BETH Blockchain School for Sustainability. Students received education in distributed ledger technology systems, coding and sustainability topics for two days and then worked on their own proofs of concept for another two days, before presenting them to the other participants. This programme was so successful that it was regularly oversubscribed, and it produced excellent use cases. Many of these students subsequently found blockchain-related jobs or stayed to write their bachelor or master thesis with us.

From the very beginning, FuturICT 2.0 has strongly emphasized the importance of outreach. As a project supported by FLAG-ERA to form new communities around an upcoming technical research field, our goal was to reach both, interested scientists as well as representatives of civil society, and leverage their interest for the themes of responsible innovation and sustainable technology.

To have an impact, we realized that we needed to reach out also to a wider public, as well as opinion leaders and governmental institutions, raising their awareness for ideas, concepts and technologies that could enable a sustainable and resilient society.

It was a logical consequence that FuturICT 2.0 moved on and established a Climate City Cup.[1] This programme encouraged individuals around the world to help tackle climate change at the city level, without waiting many years for regulations. People could collect and report data in five disciplines and collaborate to improve the sustainability of their living environment.

The first Climate City Cup was held from mid-July to mid-November 2019. The hope is to eventually run it every second year.

Following the model of the Olympic Games, the Climate City Cup encourages friendly competition, where citizens from different cities aim to develop open-source solutions to improving the sustainability of their city. The program fosters collective intelligence and provides a platform for knowledge sharing and exchange, while building bridges between communities working towards sustainable development.

The aim of the Climate City Cup 2019 was to improve urban sustainable development around the globe, with registered partner cities in Austria, Finland, Germany, India, Mali, Portugal, Slovenia, Spain, Sri Lanka, Switzerland, Turkey and the USA.

The Climate City Cup encouraged registered cities to compete in various disciplines and, thereby, advance

- air quality measurement and the reduction of pollution
- flight compensation (carbon offsetting)
- mobility and commuting practices
- circular economy
- energy consumption.

In November 2019, the first Climate City Cup awards ceremony was held in Zurich. Participants from 44 cities had contributed and generated more than tens of thousands of data points on sustainability. Moreover, an air quality sensor for crowd sensing applications was developed (see Fig. 1). And, this is just the beginning…

This book offers insights into a new way of thinking and a novel way of technology use, as it has been outlined in a technical report entitled "FuturICT 2.0: Towards a sustainable digital society with a socio-ecological finance system (Finance 4.0)".[2] Compared to the previous eBook, this edition here has been enriched by additional chapters motivating and explaining a multi-dimensional, participatory kind of money and finance system. Due to its innovative combination of money transfers

---

[1] Cf. https://web.archive.org/web/*/https://climatecitycup.org.

[2] Accessible here: http://ebook.finfour.net.

Fig. 1 Air quality sensor produced within the FuturICT 2.0 City Cup setting

with Internet of Things-based measurements, it can be seen as a new kind of real-time feedback and incentive system, which can help our economy and society to better reach its large variety of goals.

Zürich, Switzerland   Stefan Klauser

Contents

From Fiat to Crypto: The Present and Future of Money

Marcus M. Dapp

Abstract *This chapter aims to offer readers an entry point to the deep discussion of this volume and the rationale for the "Finance 4.0" system described in later chapters. What is money, why is it designed this way, and what could it become in the crypto age? The chapter contains three parts. The first part describes in rough strokes the basic functions of money and how today's fiat money system implements them. The second part offers a modest critique of the fiat money system, arguing that many problems take root in the intimate power relationship between "money and state." The final part presents two cases that address some of the shortcomings. The first is Bitcoin that infamously pursues a state-independent, decentralized conception of money. The second is Finance 4.0, a system that proposes a participatory multi-dimensional money system with built-in incentives for sustainable behavior. If more readers feel empowered to enter the public debate for a better money system in the twenty-first century, this short introduction achieved its aim.*

The Mystery of Money: What It Is and How It Works

> The study of money, above all other fields in economics,
>
> is one in which complexity is used to disguise truth or to evade truth, not to reveal it.
>
> — John Kenneth Galbraith

The author thanks Axel Apfelbacher, Mark C. Ballandies, Jürg Conzett, Carina Ines Hausladen, Dirk Helbing, and Fabian Steiner-Ligibel for helpful comments.

M. M. Dapp (✉)
ETH Zurich, Computational Social Science, Stampfenbachstrasse 48, 8092 Zurich, Switzerland
e-mail: mdapp@ethz.ch

M. M. Dapp et al. (eds.), *Finance 4.0—Towards a Socio-Ecological Finance System*,
SpringerBriefs in Applied Sciences and Technology,
https://doi.org/10.1007/978-3-030-71400-0_1

The Nature of Money

The historian Yuval Noah Harari argues that humans acquired the ability to cooperate at large scale (beyond Dunbar's number of ~150 individuals) by inventing *common myths*. Myths are stories that exist only in our collective imagination [1]. Along with nation, church, country, city, company, etc., money became one of the most influential collective imaginations in history. Its role is special because it allows transferring value across space and time. So far, money is the "most universal and most efficient system of mutual trust ever devised" [1]. All concepts making up the monetary system are such imaginations: from the value of coins and paper bills to the numbers on our bank accounts. A fascinating thought we could change the world by changing our imaginations...

As we use money every day without much thought, it is important to understand how it does work before discussing its future. Money is "the set of assets in an economy that people regularly use to buy goods and services from other people" [2]. In particular, money serves certain desired *economic functions*, which require certain *physical properties* of assets. Over time, different approaches have evolved into different *legal types* of money (Fig. 1).

To be usable as money, assets need to fulfill three economic functions [2, 3]. First, they need to be able to act as a *medium of exchange*. A medium of exchange is something that sellers accept from buyers in exchange for a good or service in the act of purchase. In order for the transaction to take place, it is crucial that the seller accepts the medium of exchange the buyer is offering for payment. Otherwise, the purchase will not take place.

Given mutual agreement, partners can split a transaction over time. Either the buyer receives the good before paying or the seller receives payment before delivering the good. For that to work, the medium of exchange needs to keep its value over that period. So, second, an asset used as money needs to be able to act as a *store of value*. The longer the time period can last, the better.

To express the value of goods in terms of other goods would be cumbersome. To say, for example: "a lunch costs the same as ten bars of chocolate, and one bar of

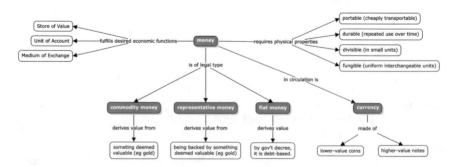

Fig. 1 Economic functions, physical properties, and legal types of money

chocolate costs the same as two packs of chewing gum." Acceptance and use of the 'money' asset must be so widespread that people also express prices in it. In other words, the asset's third function is to act as a measure, as a *unit of account*.

People have used assets with different *physical properties* over time. The physical properties determine how well an asset fulfills the economic functions and whether it ends up serving as money. Various assets served as medium of exchange in different regions at different times: cattle, shells, nails, tobacco, cotton, copper, silver, gold, and so on. Yet, not all were money. According to Hülsmann, people used the term 'money' only when a medium of exchange was "generally accepted in society" [4].

Making an asset good money requires four physical properties [5]. (1) *Fungibility* means the asset is of homogeneous texture and can be portioned in equally looking pieces. Thus, it does not matter which piece one uses (in contrast, e.g., shells and cattle come in different shapes, forms, and sizes). (2) *Portability* means the asset can be cheaply transported from one location to another because it is neither too big nor too heavy to carry. (3) *Durability* means the asset does not wear off with repeated use and changing hands over time. It also should not deteriorate on its own (e.g., tobacco will rot and silver may tarnish). (4) *Divisibility* means the asset is usable in small fractions of the same kind to represent typical values in daily transactions (e.g., silver-made coins or paper bills).

These properties subtly guided humans when deciding what goods to use as medium of exchange, store of value, and unit of account. Over millennia, people have used and accepted precious metals for payments. In particular, gold stood the literal test of time, for good reasons.[1] The advanced national economies of the last 200 years experienced an evolution of money along three different legal types (cf. Figure 1). The oldest type is *commodity money* that carries intrinsic value it derives from something deemed valuable in itself [2]. The Krugerrand, the most popular gold coin worldwide, is an example of commodity money. The gold it contains has value by itself as it is in demand for jewelry and other industrial purposes. In contrast, a modern banknote has no other use and thus no intrinsic value.

An important problem with commodity money is the danger of debasement. By replacing some fraction of a coin's precious metal content (e.g., gold or silver) with a cheaper base metal (e.g., copper or nickel), the issuer can profit from the difference between face value and metal value. Such diluted money loses value over time.

At this point, it is useful to introduce the term *inflation*. Commonly (and narrowly) defined, it is an increase in the overall level of prices [2]. To tell causes and effects apart, it is clearer to stick to the primary definition presented by Hazlitt [7]: Inflation is the increase in supply of money and credit. Each individual note and coin becomes less valuable because there are more of them available. Goods then rise in price not because goods are scarcer than before, but because notes and coins are more abundant.

Ammous [8] argues that historic periods with political regimes that avoided inflating the value of money (that was backed by precious metals) coincide with

---

[1] The Periodic Table of the Elements offers, by stepwise exclusion, a line of reasoning for gold as prime element for money [6].

prosperity for nations and citizens by increased trade, investment, and innovation. Likewise, failures to keep the monetary system 'sound' led to economic decline over time. Table 1 contrasts the periods of prosperity and decline spanning two millennia, as identified by Ammous [8].

The second type is *representative money* that has no intrinsic value, but is instead backed by a commodity, usually a precious metal like gold or silver [9]. Its origins date back to the city-states of Venice [10] and Florence [8] in thirteenth-century Italy. Goldsmiths had started to store people's gold and silver coins for safekeeping as they owned firm buildings and safes to store the precious metals for their own trade. People handed over their coins against a small fee and got a receipt on paper to represent their coins. To get them back, they had to hand in the receipt. People realized that paying with paper receipts was more comfortable than carrying heavy coins around; they hardly came back to get their coins. This marks the beginnings of modern-day *paper money* and the practice of *banking* [10].

By analogy with commodity money, representative money faces a danger of debasement (inflation) as well. Printing more "representative" banknotes than there exist precious metals on reserve to back them may lead to a shortage when many clients want to redeem their precious metal at the same time, like during a "bank run".

Representative money flourished at the end of the nineteenth, beginning of the twentieth century, when around 50 nations were on the gold standard [8]. Governments were in direct control of gold, while citizens only held paper notes redeemable for gold. Ammous argues that the reasons "a small war in Central Europe" in 1914 was able to explode into "the first global war in human history" [8] were monetary rather than geopolitical. Early in the conflict, governments suspended gold convertibility and started to finance what became an "out-of-control arms race" [11]. Unlike during previous wars, they could now access the wealth of the entire population rather than just the government treasuries, which in the past set a natural limit to the size of wars. Without this possibility, World War I would have been much smaller in scope and duration, Ammous argues [8].

As all currencies had lost in value because of war financing, it was politically difficult to re-enter the gold standard [11]. It would have required to admit that governments significantly devalued the currency, e.g., down to 51% of prewar levels for losing power Germany. Therefore, countries took the "easier path" of currency debasement to solve their economic problems. Germany used inflation to pay for the large reparations stemming from the Treaty of Versailles—which promptly led to the infamous hyperinflation in Germany in 1922/1923, paving the way to the Nazi regime and World War II [11]. The USA also engaged in inflationary monetary policy in the 1920s, leading to the infamous October 1929 stock market crash and the decade-long Great Depression, which only ceased when the USA entered World War II in 1940. Within five years, state-imposed war production made unemployment "disappear" into the military and increased state expenses by a factor of ten [11].

The international system based on the gold standard was no longer functional, and war and economic devastation were rampant. Ammous [8] argues that money

Table 1 Choice of monetary system influences prosperity and decline of societies over time (summarized after [8])

Time span	Prospering periods	Declining periods
ca. 50 BCE	Roman Republic under Julius Caesar (silver *denarius* and gold *aureus* with stable metal content)	
50–300 BC	Roman Empire under Nero, Caracalla, and Diocletian (significant debasement of aureus and denarius through metal content reduction leads to overspending and inflation; new *solidus* at only half the gold content of aureus)	
3rd–4th C	Constantine the Great builds Byzantium and brings gold solidus to the East	
5th–15th C		Dark Ages in the West: Gold gets gradually accumulated by feudal lords through taxation and inflation, leaving the peasantry to use worthless coins of abundant *copper* and *bronze*
3rd–15th C	Prosperity in the East: Byzantine Empire lasts 1000 years. It is backed by solidus, now renamed to *bezant*. The bezant is used over centuries, up to today as the *Islamic dinar*	
1250–1300	City-states create own coins, the *Ducat*: 1252 Genoa (gold *genovino*), Florence (gold *fiorino, florin*), 1284 Venice (gold *ducato d'oro*), heralding the transition from the Dark Age to the Renaissance	
1814–1914	For a few decades, many nations are on a *gold standard*, easing international trade during La Belle Époque, the "greatest period of human flourishing, innovation (…) the world has ever witnessed" [8]	
1914–1945		World War I, followed by several economic depressions, followed by World War II, ushers in the era of modern "government money" [8]

gradually turned into a politically controlled instrument rather than a market-priced commodity.

It was John Maynard Keynes who, in 1939, delivered the theoretical argument to legitimize further government intervention [12]. Keynes argued in favor of *continued spending* in the economy (high aggregate demand, including government spending) as it determines the overall level of economic activity. Inadequate aggregate demand, in contrast, could lead to prolonged periods of high unemployment. He argued for *fiscal and monetary policies* to mitigate the adverse effects during economic recessions and depressions, and restraint during prosperous times [12]. Table 2 shows the series of regulations and international agreements that unfolded to implement Keynes' ideas.

Table 2 Drift from representative money to fiat money (own research)

1913	US Federal Reserve Act. Establishment of the Federal Reserve system (FED) [11]
1922	Genoa Conference establishes US dollar and British pound as reserve currencies for other countries, next to gold [13]
1929	US stock market crash leads to the decade-long Great Depression period [11]
1930	Bank of International Settlement (BIS) is established to facilitate reparations imposed on Germany by the Treaty of Versailles after World War I. Today's role is to foster monetary and financial cooperation and serve as a "bank for central banks" (cf. footnote 5)
1933	Newly elected US President Roosevelt initiates "New Deal" program to counter the Great Depression [14] Roosevelt issues Executive Order No. 6102 to "prohibit the hoarding of gold coin, gold bullion, and gold certificates within the continental United States", demanding US citizens to sell their gold at 20.67 USD per ounce to the US Treasury[2]
1934	US Gold Reserve Act. Among its wide-ranging provisions are: (1) confiscation of all gold owned by the FED and transfer to the US Department of Treasury, (2) prohibition to redeem dollar bills for gold, (3) establishment of the Exchange Stabilization Fund to control the dollar price without the FED, (4) authorization of the president to set a new price of gold by proclamation (sic!) [15]. The new price is 35 USD per ounce, i.e. 69% higher
1944	Agreement on the Bretton Woods System [8, 16]: (1) The US dollar becomes global reserve currency with fixed exchange rates for other central banks. Currencies are convertible to USD, and (only) the USD is convertible to gold. For that, US buys gold from other countries at 35 USD per ounce. The "fixed" exchange rates can be altered to address "fundamental disequilibrium" (2) The International Monetary Fund (IMF) is established to coordinate the global group of central banks on exchange rate stability (3) The International Bank for Reconstruction and Development (today World Bank Group) is established to provide financial assistance for post World War II reconstruction and economic development
1971	US President Nixon announces unilateral measures to address domestic inflation and unemployment as well as the threat of an international gold run on the US[3] (1) He suspends international gold convertibility for central banks, thus halting the Bretton Woods Agreement. (2) He freezes prices and wages for 90 days and raises tariff on all dutiable imports by an extra ten percent.

With the Bretton Woods agreement, the world had a system of fixed currency exchange rates, with the US dollar at the center as the global reserve currency, and the only one backed by gold reserves, deposited by all nations in Fort Knox. In 1971, however, US President Nixon faced a difficult situation: a high domestic unemployment and inflation rate combined with the fact that more foreign-held dollars circulated outside its borders than the US had gold reserves required action. In a swift unilateral move, Nixon announced national wage and price controls and the end of the convertibility of US dollars to gold for other countries. The announcement effectively made the Bretton Woods Agreement obsolete [11]. The "Nixon shock" decoupled the US dollar (and with it all other currencies) from the gold standard and marked the departure from representative money.

With the third type of money, *fiat money,* we take a final step away from grounding money in physical valuable assets as fiat money is not redeemable in gold anymore. Due to its omnipresence today, it deserves its own section.

The Fiat Money System

Fiat money is the monetary system that has gradually developed over the last few centuries and has become the globally dominant system over the last few decades. A widely used student textbook of economics defines it as "money without intrinsic value that is used as money because of government decree" [2]. In other words, printed notes and minted coins (and bank deposits) only have value because the government declared them "legal tender" to discharge debt. The government demands tax payments in legal tender, thus creating a continuous demand for its money.

The ultimate backing of the money monopoly is military state power. *"Nowadays, the political power uses its power of coercion to impose a monopoly on the production and circulation of money, which in particular implies the existence of a 'legal tender', that is, a prohibition on currencies other than the 'national' currency"* [17]. A national currency directs and enforces monetary policy in the domestic economy and constitutes an instrument of geopolitical power among nations. Controlling the dominant currency yields considerable benefits to the respective state like "the ability to issue securities that are always in high demand by the rest of the world" [18]. In 2020, the world is still accepting the US dollar as its reserve currency, despite tensions in trade relations and rivalry between the USA and the Republic of China.

Controlling money means primarily controlling the money supply. Figure 2 illustrates the entities and mechanisms involved in the domestic process of fiat money creation in a simplified form.

The *macro-mechanism* of fiat money creation is an interplay between fiscal and monetary policy, managed by an institutional setup consisting of the government

---

[2]Cf. https://www.presidency.ucsb.edu/documents/executive-order-6102-requiring-gold-coin-gold-bullion-and-gold-certificates-be-delivered

[3]Cf. https://www.federalreservehistory.org/essays/gold-convertibility-ends

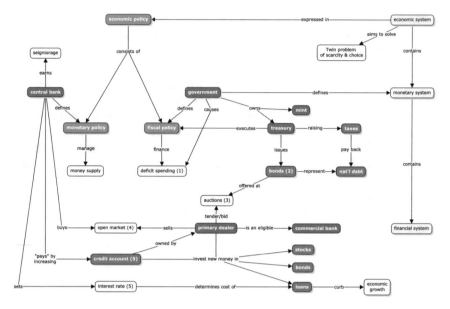

Fig. 2 Creating fiat money is an intricate interplay between fiscal and monetary policy

treasury, the central bank, and commercial banks. The mechanism comprises five steps (Fig. 2). (1) It starts with *deficit spending*, which means the government needs to spend more money than it currently has, maybe because of political promises made before an election. Government has two options to address deficit spending. One of the two options (leaving the third, defaulting on the debt, aside) is fiscal policy. Yet, raising taxes is usually an unpopular move for an elected government. (2) Thus remains the option to borrow money by *issuing government bonds*. As bonds are loans with a fixed interest rate, the government effectively commits current and future taxpayers to new, additional national debt. (3) To generate income, the government treasury holds *bond auctions*, in which only a selected group of commercial banks ("primary dealers") is allowed to tender, i.e., to make bids. The banks bid to buy parts of the national debt to earn interest with it. (4) In so-called *open market operations*, the central bank can purchase specific types of securities in the open market, directly from other market players. As counterparts in these open market operations, commercial banks sell these bonds to the central bank, at a profit. (5) To pay, the central bank simply "use[s] the computer to mark up" the *credit account* of the respective primary dealer on its balance sheet, thus calling new money into existence in a way "much more akin to printing money than it is to borrowing" [19].

Technically, the central bank is buying government bonds through "open market operations" (US Federal Reserve) or "asset purchase programs" (European Central Bank). In the case of the European Central Bank, one of currently five different asset purchase programs, the "Public Sector Purchase Program (PSPP)", deals with government-issued bonds.[4]

The *micro-mechanism* for creating money involves commercial banks and their clients. To describe it, we need to continue the story of the Venetian goldsmiths from the previous section. Realizing that most people left their precious metal coins with them for the convenience of paper receipts, some "astute goldsmiths" started to issue *more* receipts than they had coins in store. "[T]hey began to issue more money than they actually held in coins" [10] and increased their income without increasing reserves. This deliberate act became common practice today, known as *fractional reserve banking*: Banks do not need to keep 100% of clients' deposits as reserve, but only a fraction. Since January 2012, the reserve ratio in the euro area is only 1% [20].

By converting dormant deposit money into loans, banks create new money. Fractional reserve banking permits banks to use idle deposits to generate additional interest returns on the loans issued. "[W]henever a bank makes a loan, it simultaneously creates a matching deposit in the borrower's bank account, thereby creating new money" [21]. For example, with 1 million of client money and a reserve requirement of 10%, a bank can hand out ten loans each of size 1 million, thus creating 9 million in additional deposit money.

This logic rests on the assumption that clients will never withdraw all their deposits at the same time. Of course, this assumption may break during crises and lead to bank runs—a situation when a bank, in order to be able to pay out many deposits, asks many clients to repay their loans quickly. If the clients are unable to do so, the bank gets into trouble.[5] Thus, the circle closes because one of the main tasks of modern central banks is to *prevent* such crises and ensure monetary stability among other objectives, as summarized by Ugolini [23]:

> Nowadays, central bankers agree in acknowledging that they are entrusted two main (possibly conflicting) tasks: securing financial stability and monetary stability. The former task consists of the provision of the microeconomic central banking functions: the management of the payment system, lending of last resort, and banking supervision. The latter task consists of the provision of the macroeconomic central banking functions: the issuance of money and the conduct of monetary policy.

Reflecting on these mechanisms of creating fiat money leads to a number of critical remarks.

---

[4]Cf. https://www.ecb.europa.eu/mopo/implement/omt/html/index.en.html.

[5]The Basel Committee on Banking Supervision (BCBS) as part of the Bank for International Settlement (BIS) is composed of central banks from 28 jurisdictions. It issues the "Basel Accords", a set of recommendations on banking supervision and risk management, regulating minimum capital requirements including risk weights for asset classes. "Basel III", intended as a response to the Global Financial Crisis 2008/2009, was agreed in 2010 to put stricter risk management metrics for banks by 2015. It was extended repeatedly and will, most recently because of COVID-19, not be implemented earlier than 2023, over a decade later [22].

A Modest Critique of Money

Analyzing the mechanisms of the fiat monetary system reveals several issues that warrant a closer look. The following critique cannot be exhaustive, but aims to raise some issues that are particularly relevant with regard to the proposals laid out in the last section and the main chapter on "Finance 4.0" of this volume.

Fiat Money Is Debt-Based

Fiat money is created as debt in the moment of issuing loans [24]. A new asset purchase by a central bank or a new loan by a commercial bank increases the money supply in a subtle way that is invisible for most people. "Debt-based" means that an amount someone owns represents an equal amount of debt for someone else in the system. Hence, creating new money means creating new debt. Nations with fiat money systems tend to accumulate debt over time.[6] Creating money from "thin air" also permits banks (and governments) to gain excessive financial and political power in relation to all other members of society. Moreover, the fiat money system misleads the world to live beyond its means and thus expedites the sustainability crisis.

How to reduce debt? According to Dalio [25], governments have four options to reduce debt and debt service: (1) austerity policy (i.e., spending less); (2) debt defaults/restructuring; (3) the central bank creating money, making purchases or providing guarantees; (4) redistributing money and credit from "those who have more than they need to those who have less."

The first two options are unpopular among governments as they are hard to explain to voters. A policy of austerity can be devastating as falling prices may lead to a downward feedback cycle of falling asset prices and increasing unemployment ("deflationary shock"), which may end in debt defaults of many businesses. The fourth option, to transfer money/credit between stakeholder groups, is also delicate as powerful voter groups may lose out and thus fight the policy. For officials aiming for re-election, this is a problematic situation. Besides, there are often legal issues when governments interfere with private property.

This leaves governments with the third option: "creating money" to finance the debts as discussed in the previous section. Under normal circumstances, the typical inflation target hovers around 2% (a coincidental and arbitrary number [26]), which is a money creation rate that only experts recognize. Most voters do not realize the continuous price increases although at this 2% rate prices double every 35 years. The consequence is an ever increasing amount of government debt, for which all citizens need to pay. Where do the countries stand today? The Managing Director

---

[6]In 2012, the EU created the 'European Stability Mechanism', an intergovernmental organization in Luxembourg, with the mission to provide financial assistance in the form of 'ESM loans' to member countries experiencing financing problems, like Cyprus and Greece in the past. cf. https://www.esm.europa.eu/assistance/lending-toolkit.

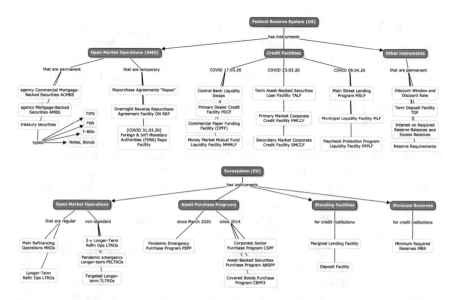

Fig. 3 Arsenal of central banking instruments of Federal Reserve System and Eurosystem

of the International Monetary Fund (IMF) stated that *global public debt* will reach a "record-high of about 100 percent of GDP in 2020" [27].

Distortion of Price Signals

As illustrated for the Federal Reserve System[7] and the Eurosystem[8] in Fig. 3, analyzing the opaque arsenal of central bank instruments is a staggering experience. Most people would have a hard time realizing and understanding the implications of running these complicated structures.

---

[7] For the Federal Reserve System instruments, cf. https://www.federalreserve.gov/monetarypolicy/policytools.htm.

[8] For the Eurosystem instruments, cf. https://www.ecb.europa.eu/mopo/implement/omt/html/index.en.html.

End of October 2020, the stock of all asset purchase programs managed by the Eurosystem stood at 3,470 trillion EUR, while the balance sheet of the Federal Reserve stood at 7,157 trillion USD. In other words, each of the many instruments has the potential to inject hundreds of billions into the monetary system.[9] It is important to understand that all this new money is created as credit (debt) *without* an equivalent increase in the production of goods and services in the real economy. Channeling so much new money into the system leads to an upward pressure on price levels in the market, because the additional money available is not matched by more goods and services. Hence, assets, goods, and services are becoming more expensive in terms of monetary units (USD, EUR, etc.) to be spent for consuming them or investing into them, solely because the monetary base is inflated without any change in the real economic conditions. From January 2009 to September 2020, the Consumer Price Index[10] for urban consumers in the US (CPI) rose by 23% and the Harmonized Index of Consumer Prices in the EU (HICP) by 19%.[11]

Economies are complex socioeconomic networks with nonlinear relationships, i.e., causes and effects are not proportional to each other [28]. The effect the central bank has on employment decisions by businesses via influencing the conditions for commercial bank loans is one example for such a nonlinear relationship. However, the assumed logic—cheaper loans lead to investments and higher levels of employment—may not work as intended. Rather, one may find "jumpy", nonlinear behavior for a variety of reasons: (i) banks may not pass the money on as loans, but channel it to other markets such as stocks; (ii) businesses may not take out loans to avoid additional debt in difficult times; or (iii) businesses may take out loans but not use them to keep staff or expand, but to buy back shares. When making such decisions, banks and businesses may take "private" information (unknown and unknowable to the central bank) into consideration and decide in unintended ways. Anything between none and all three options may happen at the same time, leading to seemingly contradictory effects. For example, some businesses may go insolvent[12] for lack of orders, while excess money flows into asset markets. Thus, inflated prices may become "visible" outside consumer price indices: in rising stock prices, rising gold and silver prices, or rising real estate prices.

---

[9]For the ECB figure cf. previous footnote plus figure from https://www.ecb.europa.eu/mopo/imp lement/pepp/html/index.en.html. For the FED figure cf. https://www.federalreserve.gov/monetaryp olicy/bst_recenttrends.htm.

[10]Consumer price indexing, the official metric for inflation, is challenged because the composition of the reference basket of goods, dynamic adjustments, etc. significantly influence the price tracking. In contrast, crowd-sourced indices like the Chapwood Index for the US show consistent higher inflation rates: https://chapwoodindex.com/. For an introduction to the debate, see: https://www.inv estopedia.com/articles/07/consumerpriceindex.asp.

[11]For the US cf. https://fred.stlouisfed.org/series/CPIAUCSL, for the EU cf. https://sdw.ecb.eur opa.eu/.

[12]Or, they may *not* go insolvent but turn into so-called "zombie companies", unable to pay the interest on their loans, but kept alive by very low interest rates and/or government support. About 16-36% of companies in the EU in 2019 [29] and about 20% in the US in 2020 [30] are considered to be zombie companies. Directing funds away from healthy companies is a major concern as it may depress employment and growth in the future.

It is very hard to predict and control how central bank money ends up being used. In other words, central banks pursue this approach without knowing when they reach a tipping point that causes the system to shift to a new regime [28]. Such a new regime could be hyperinflation, an asset bubble burst, or a wave of insolvencies and unemployment. All of them may lead to large fractions of the general public and financial markets to lose trust in the stability of the national currency, resulting in bank runs and large declines in currency value (relative to other currencies or assets). Consequently, the acceptance of money in exchange for goods or services deteriorates and the common myth of money starts to collapse [1]. Evaluating empirical data on such tipping points is sobering. Since 1800, *bank runs* (affecting one bank), *bank panics* (affecting several banks), or *banking crises* (affecting entire countries) are happening every 7–10 years on average, with no significant difference between advanced economies and emerging markets [31].

Finally, as this additional money needs to enter the economy at some point and then start moving from one market participant to the next, the so-called "Cantillon effect" plays out [32]. The first users of new money can still use it to buy goods at unchanged prices. However, with each market transaction, the information about the new money spreads in the markets and prices gradually adjust. In other words, there is a re-allocation of resources "in favor of those economic agents that receive the new money first" [32]. The question then is: who in society benefits from new money first?

Overall, increasing the money supply in the absence of an increase in economic activity causes distortions in the price levels and puts a large group of market participants in difficult positions.

The Economy Is Complex, Not Just Complicated

From a systems science perspective, the main question is: *How do we think a small group of people with a narrow set of goals and a one-dimensional metric can steer a complex economic network consisting of millions of individuals, to a state of comprehensive well-being for the majority?*

Ad "small group": The Governing Council of the Eurosystem consists of 22, the Federal Open Market Committee of the FED of 12 individuals [33]. These two groups are steering the economic lives of 330.5 million inhabitants in 52 US states and 447.7 million inhabitants in 27 EU countries.[13] No matter how much staff assigned or which key metrics used, it seems to be impossible for 34 humans to get a sufficiently deep understanding of these enormous (and enormously diverse) economies in order to decide top-down what the single best monetary policy is for everyone.

Ad "narrow goals": Contemporary economics puts an undue focus on one goal – monetary efficiency – at the neglect of health, sustainability, happiness, well-being,

---

[13]Cf. https://www.census.gov/ and https://www.statista.com/statistics/253372/total-population-of-the-european-union-eu/.

and other societal goals many deem important [24]. The FED's monetary policy is "to promote maximum employment, stable prices, and moderate long-term interest rates in the US. economy" [34]. The primary objective of the ECB's monetary policy is to maintain price stability. The ECB aims at inflation rates of "below, but close to, 2% over the medium term" [35]. In other words, the primary goal of central banks is to mitigate price rise, i.e., inflation, which is the key *design feature* of a fiat money system in the first place. This narrow goal, only to make the fiat money system work, stands against the "Agenda 2030", a holistic set of 17 goals aiming at global sustainable development, unanimously adopted by 193 member states of the United Nations in 2015 [36]. Yet, the monetary system, which dominates world affairs, lacks transparency, democratic governance and legitimacy. How is this possible?

Ad "one control metric": Using a one-dimensional metric for decision-making and resource allocation is dangerous and can considerably affect the functioning of the overall system of society. Other complex systems use diverse variables, i.e., a multi-dimensional approach, to steer the entire system [37, 38]. The human body, for example, uses several mechanisms (nervous system, hormone system, immune system, etc.) to keep the overall organism well-performing, where even the brain does not control all processes (cf. the chapter on "Qualified Money" in this volume). In the same vein, steering modern complex economies may require more complex, multi-dimensional feedback mechanisms for a self-organization of society towards overall prosperity and well-being [39].

Accordingly, Dosi and Roventini [40] make the case for "agent-based models as the standard way of theorizing in macroeconomics". They see the economy as a complex evolving system, an ecology populated by heterogeneous agents, whose far-from-equilibrium interactions continuously change the structure of the system.

In closing, I would briefly like to mention that the failure of the majority of economists to adequately predict the financial crisis 2008/2009 has caused a large-scale critical discourse within the economics discipline [41, 42]. Felber presents a collection of wide-ranging criticisms that go as far as accusing the economic profession of mathematical fetish and "physics envy", of theory monoculture and narrowness in teaching [43]. As a consequence, an international student initiative for "Pluralism in Economics"[14] has formed in 2014, consisting of 82 associations of economics students from 31 countries. It calls for an "overhaul of the way their subject is taught" [44]. The dominance of narrow free-market theories at top universities, it claims, harms the world's ability to confront challenges like financial stability and climate change.

Separation of State and Money in the Digital Age

Central banks have limited control over how newly issued money is used (cf. the discussion on 'price signals' above). This is the main argument they put forward

---

[14]Cf. http://www.isipe.net/.

in favor of "central bank issued digital currencies (CBDC)". Several institutions published reports on CBDC in 2020 [45–49]. Note, however, that digital currencies in this context and cryptocurrencies as discussed further below are entirely different concepts.

According to the International Monetary Fund (IMF), CBDC would give central banks a "fast and direct means to provide fiscal assistance to vulnerable populations during the emergency, including to the unbanked" [49]. CBDC allows injecting new money directly into (newly created) central bank accounts for businesses and citizens. The money could bypass the banking system, which is believed to reduce the liquidity squeeze short-term and the dangers of inflation long-term.

Central banks see several advantages of digital currencies: (1) faster and cheaper payment processing as large parts of the banking industry could be circumvented; (2) more effective policy measures because of better targeting of groups and individuals; (3) easier introduction of unpopular measures such as negative interest rates, from which citizens could not escape as cash withdrawals would cease to exist, thus rendering bank runs impossible.

It is important, however, to understand the severe implications of CBDC for citizens. (1) It will be possible to track *all* transactions of *all* citizens and businesses in real time. Making anonymous cash payments will be impossible, even for completely legal transactions, thereby threaten privacy rights. (2) Governments can use transaction data to personalize fiscal policies (e.g., automatic taxation) and fiscal benefits (e.g., automatic basic income). Subjugating these activities under democratic accountability processes will be hard. The door for behavioral economists to nudge, manipulate, or even prevent transactions for certain people will be wide open.

A new *Surveillance Monetarism* may arise, akin to Surveillance Capitalism [50], only with different actors. Governments or central banks may analyze citizens and influence their behavior with programmable CBDC and Artificial Intelligence. They will become even more capable to track citizens and to conceal operations within the already opaque fiat money system.

This new capability may have geopolitical implications when the CBDC is issued by a large economic power (e.g., China, USA, EU). They may pressure trading partners to accept their CBDC as they do with fiat currency today.[15] In addition, the foreign CBDC will put the partner countries' citizens at risk of being monitored by a foreign power. Thus, large and powerful 'suppliers' of a CBDC may be at an advantage in bargaining monetary hegemony.

In his treatise against cash, Rogoff [51] presents a devious plan for ways that governments can use to lure the population into letting go of cash. His recommendations for phasing out paper currency are [51]: (1) make it more difficult to engage in anonymous untraceable transactions repeatedly and on a large scale; (2) stretch the transition phase over 10–15 years to avoid excessive disruptions and give institutions and people time to adapt; (3) give incentives to opt-in like free smartphones and free accounts.

---

[15]The effect, called "Dollarization" or "Euroization", is an example of currency substitution that can happen with CBDC for similar reasons, but much more efficient.

However, Rogoff's conception of essential aspects of cryptocurrencies in general and Bitcoin in particular has flaws [51], which is a reason for hope that there will be a more positive 'future of money.' When it becomes clearer to more people, how the current monetary system perpetuates disadvantages for a majority of citizens and businesses, while new systems would offer advantages for many or all, history may take another turn this time. In fact, the promise of 'crypto money' is to democratize the creation and management of money in society.

The Many Futures of Money

I don't believe we shall ever have a good money again before we take the thing out of the hands of government, that is, we can't take it violently out of the hands of government, all we can do is by some sly roundabout way introduce something that they can't stop.

—F.A. Hayek (1984)

The goal of my final section is to introduce new ways of thinking and designing monetary systems in order to stretch the imagination for what might be possible. I personally expect a greater diversity of digital incentive systems ('crypto monies') in the future.

To illustrate the spectrum, let me introduce and discuss only two examples here. Both share a few commonalities: (i) They differ significantly from the dominant fiat money system, albeit in different ways; (ii) both would not be possible without distributed ledgers, blockchain technology, and smart contracts; (iii) both share the unconventional idea that money can and should be democratic.

The two examples also differ in significant ways from each other: (i) One aims for 'world dominance' while the other is explicitly complementary in nature; (ii) one implies a winner-takes-all dynamic, while the other foresees a plurality of monies for different purposes; (iii) one is criticized for its energy consumption, while the other has sustainability at its core; (iv) one is in productive use already for a decade, while the other is still at the level of a research and demonstration project.

Bitcoin, a Radical Idea Refusing to Die

The root problem with conventional currency is all the trust that's required to make it work. The central banks must be trusted not to debase the currency, but the history of fiat currencies is full of breaches of that trust.

—Satoshi Nakamoto (anonymous inventor of Bitcoin)

The main question regarding Bitcoin, the oldest cryptocurrency project (and largest in monetary terms), is not, where the Bitcoin price will go. It is rather, why is Bitcoin still alive in 2020 and why do people think it is even valuable?

Twelve years ago, the Bitcoin project started with a white paper and a tiny piece of software code serving as a proof of concept [52]. It took a while until the cryptography community fully appreciated its design and started to contribute open-source code and to develop the underlying technical system. Against all odds, what started as a software network experiment of a few cryptography nerds, ended up becoming a global phenomenon valued at 320 billion USD as of this writing (November 2020). A few numbers for comparison: (1) This is more than the Gross Domestic Product of 80% of the 195 countries monitored by the IMF [53]; (2) to replace the "inefficient global foreign exchange market" [8], Bitcoin would need to be valued in the vicinity of 5 trillion USD or a factor of 15 higher; (3) to reach gold's market value, Bitcoin's valuation would need to reach 8.4 trillion USD or 26 times its current value [54]. These factors seem enormous and unattainable. Yet, over the last decade, the valuation grew from 0.01 USD to 10'000 USD per bitcoin. That is a factor of 1'000'000.[16] Why do people think Bitcoin deserves this valuation?

Note how the *monetary properties* of the Bitcoin system contradict those of the fiat money system. First, consider its "absolute scarcity" in supply [8]. Roughly every ten minutes, a new block of transactions is created and the miner receives a reward called "block subsidy". Starting with 50 bitcoin initially, this block subsidy is halved every 210'000 blocks. As the number of halvings is limited to 64 (of which only 3 have passed so far), the overall sum will approach but never exceed 21'000'000 bitcoin. This hard cap is the exact opposite of the ever-increasing money supply in the fiat money system.

Second, consider its "unforgeable costliness" of creation [55]. Similar to gold mining, the process of creating new bitcoin needs a proof requiring a significant and usually increasing amount of computing work to be done. And there are no shortcuts: The "proof of work" algorithm is a contest to guess a large number with certain characteristics (called a "hash") for which no faster mathematical method than trial-and-error is known. At the time of writing, the Bitcoin network needs to calculate and test approx. 10^{18} hashes per second to construct a new valid block within ten minutes. Dissimilar to gold, the difficulty level increases with increasing computing capacity, while the rewards decrease over time (due to the halving mentioned above). Using a stock-to-flow model, the prediction is that from 2024 onward, Bitcoin will be harder to "mine" and thus grow less in supply than gold that has been used as a store of value for millennia [56].

So, what are Bitcoin's key properties that allowed it to become such a radically different monetary system? People typically ascribe a set of properties to Bitcoin similar to the ones listed in Table 3.

To fully understand Bitcoin, it is crucial to acknowledge the fact that only some properties are *design properties*, consciously determined by the Bitcoin developers at the outset of the project. Some others (marked with * in Table 3) are *emergent properties* of the complex system that Bitcoin represents. The latter have not been

---

[16]It is an interesting design fact that Bitcoin has not two digits like most fiat currencies, but eight. That means that 100,000,000 Satoshis (the smallest unit) make 1 BTC. In other words, Bitcoin is many orders of magnitude more divisible than any money humans ever used.

Table 3 List of properties typically ascribed to the Bitcoin system

Open: The Bitcoin software is free and open source	**Borderless**: Being a global network, national borders can not restrict transactions
Decentralized*: Bitcoin's governance is not hierarchical	**Distributed**: The underlying network is peer-to-peer rather than a client/server architecture
Permissionless: There are no barriers to using Bitcoin	**Censorship resistant:** Neither transactions nor users can be blocked
Immutable*: The Bitcoin ledger storing all transactions cannot be modified unilaterally in retrospect	**Trustless***: Performing transactions on the network requires no trusted third parties

consciously planned for (nor could they). However, they have been spontaneously emerging over time because of the monetary properties described above. This allowed a specific incentive system between users and miners in the network to self-organize.

Immutable: Bitcoin's monetary policy dictates how new bitcoin come into existence. Some critics argue that software developers could simply change the software code, and then, Bitcoin would behave differently, have no hard cap, different block subsidies, etc. Yet, getting a different software code accepted into the official code repository is not straightforward at all. Bitcoin's code is open-source software. That means if developers disagree with the direction the project is taking, they can always take a copy of the code base and create an alternative path. Such departures, called forks, usually mean a split (and, thus, a weakening) of the currency—and of the community. Despite several forks (Bitcoin Cash, Bitcoin Satoshi's Vision, Bitcoin Gold, and others), Bitcoin is still, by far, the most valued cryptocurrency network.

What would it take to rally the majority of the network nodes behind a software change to switch to a different monetary policy? In the case of increasing the number of bitcoin or introducing inflation, it would require to convince a majority of Bitcoin nodes to alter the network *against* their financial interests. This is unlikely, because neither users nor miners have an incentive to change the Bitcoin code to create more bitcoin retrospectively and thus inflate the existing supply (collectively owned by them).

Trustless: Through the combination of mining rewards and transaction fees, miners have a monetary incentive to process transaction blocks, thus keeping the network secure, alive and functioning as users expect it: this allows them to transact digitally world-wide without the need for any intermediaries. Cheating (e.g., by double spending bitcoin) became more difficult over time as it requires to control more than half of the immense computing power needed to mine transaction blocks.

Decentralized: Over time and all over the world, the Bitcoin system attracted an increasing number of participants, users, and miners to the network. The Bitcoin network currently consists of roughly 10'000 listening nodes worldwide.

25% of them do not reveal their country location.[17] Mining needs initial investments, but anyone can start to run their own full node and support the Bitcoin network.

Altogether, Bitcoin's emergent properties make it a radically different monetary system from what humans have known so far. They are also the cause for why it is becoming harder to change Bitcoin's inner workings, the longer it lives.

Now, assuming its design will remain stable, what could Bitcoin become like in the future? If the trajectory of absolute scarcity of supply, unforgeable costliness of creation, and immutable monetary policy will remain stable, Bitcoin may challenge the global economic order in a couple of years [57]. If it continues to survive, Bitcoin may become the first instance of "sound money" as theorized by Austrian Economics [8, 58] or "ideal money" as proposed by Nash [59].

At some point, some governments may consider using Bitcoin due to high national debt or geopolitical challenges, e.g., surveillance monetarism imposed by a foreign CBDC. They may find a hard, stable asset, which is less prone to international geopolitics, to be more attractive than to continue defending their national currency. Bitcoin could also become attractive for central banks to hold as a complementary reserve asset to gold.

In 2020, the corporate sector has been starting to move into Bitcoin. The first few publicly traded companies announced to store large sums of treasury funds in bitcoin in order to reduce risk exposure to fiat currencies.[18]

So, what is it that Bitcoin is accomplishing? In the words of Bratton: *"If nothing else, Bitcoin has made money into a general design problem, as it should be, and not just the design of financial products or the look of paper bills, but of vessel abstractions of time, debt, work, and prestige"* [60].

To illustrate the wide spectrum of cryptocurrency designs, let me now introduce another design proposal, which is the result of rethinking how new kinds of money could be used to promote inclusive socio-ecological development – the main topic of this volume.

Finance 4.0, a Socio-Ecological Financial System

We started from the working hypothesis that at the core of most societal problems are non-sustainable practices and misaligned incentive schemes. Currently, a boundless, globalized economy is systematically creating negative externalities. This is not being sanctioned sufficiently, because globalized regulation is not effective enough. The monetary system adds to that by not setting the required incentives from within as it feeds on two human traits: the cognitive bias to prefer a reward that arrives sooner over one that arrives later ("hyperbolic discounting" or "low time preference") and

---

[17]Cf. statistics and map of listening nodes on: https://bitnodes.io/. The number of full nodes is not directly measurable, but estimated to be up to ten times larger.

[18]Cf. https://bitcointreasuries.org/ for a curated list.

the inability of properly comprehending the long-term outcomes of an action while deciding ("temporal myopia") [61].

Today's monetary system leads to a preference of short-term thinking and acting, thereby overlooking or ignoring the long-term consequences. Therefore, we need to re-arrange our societal incentive systems toward *long-termism:* "[f]rom a global perspective, what matters most (in expectation) is that we do what is best (in expectation) for the general trajectory along which our descendants develop over the coming millions, billions, and trillions of years" [62].

What is needed is monetary innovation, experimentation, and competition to create a new relationship between money and sustainable practice. The good news is: We already have parallel, state-independent complementary currency systems:[19] Since the 1980s, approx. 3'500 to 4'500 such systems have been recorded in more than 50 countries [10, 63].

If complementary currencies, i.e., alternatives to the current system, provide evidence of successfully addressing some societal challenges, why are they not more researched, discussed, and written about in mainstream economics? Hülsmann argues that economists, too, act within an incentive system. While "championing government involvement in money and banking pays the bills, promoting the opposite agenda shuts the doors to an academic career. No consistent economist could expect monetary economists to lead campaigns against central banks and paper money" [4, 24].

Nevertheless, I would like to argue that money should aim at mitigating the problem of negative externalities and at providing incentives toward sustainable practice.

The current monetary system only optimizes for one goal—profit maximization. Instead of optimizing only for "more money", while neglecting other vital goals, the monetary system should enable many feedback loops, to reflect the multitude of goals humans have. Letting people create their own "monies" around these goals will foster self-organization of markets for different externalities and enable the co-evolution of different, distinct incentive systems (cf. the chapters on Qualified Money and Finance 4.0 in this volume).

Using tokens to represent incentives is a concept from psychology that suggests that incentive systems with tokens work best when the tokens are abstract, provide immediate feedback, and lead to a bigger, longer-term reinforcer [64]. However, to avoid nudging [65] and the dangers of top-down manipulation [66], it is important that users are *self-sovereign* in creating and deciding on the actions they want to incentivize and the tokens they want to use.

Many environmental and social problems are an example of a "commons dilemma, a social situation in which a collective cost or risk is generated via the combined negative externalities of numerous individuals who act rather independently from

---

[19]They are defined as a "unit (or system) of account that complements the official currency and has been developed by a group of agents (individuals, economic and social structures, local authorities or banks) that has formed a local network with a view to accounting for and regulating exchanges of goods and services" [63].

one another" [67]. Elinor Ostrom laid seminal groundwork by presenting principles to overcome the commons dilemma by a common-pool resource management that is effective for small, interconnected communities [68]. Scaling these to large, anonymous networks, however, is a challenge, that required polycentric approaches in the past.

The emergence of distributed ledger technology and the token engineering/cryptoeconomics discipline now allows us to implement and collectively coordinate such sociotechnical complex systems at scale. The decentralization and immutability of "blockchains" and "smart contracts" enable us to co-design and co-monitor the rules needed to make the network produce positive action [69].

Put differently, cryptoeconomics has the potential to create a scalable peer-to-peer governance model for managing the commons. Smart incentive design could be a way to encourage more long-term thinking and succeed by establishing mechanisms that reward long-term, sustainable behaviors on the scale of the Internet.

Rethinking the notions of value and money and shifting toward long-term thinking are necessary to create the social ecosystems – Harari's "collective imaginations" [1] – that can collaboratively change our world from an extractive to a regenerative one. Table 4 contrasts the two paradigms in terms of system goals, structure, and rules.

The core idea of the Finance 4.0 system, which will be detailed in the corresponding chapter in this volume, is to propose design principles and a technological infrastructure for a socio-ecological finance system that aims to maintain the commons and reduces negative externalities. Hence, the core *design principles* of the Finance 4.0 system are:

- The system encourages a multi-dimensional incentive design to address different externalities and strengthen the commons by focusing on socio-ecological goals.
- The system allows for and encourages the bottom-up creation of tokens to distribute the power to design and create money.

Table 4 Contrasting the paradigm of the current financial system with the Finance 4.0 system

Current financial system	Finance 4.0 system
System goals are one-dimensional (profit maximization) and self-referential (targets, e.g., money supply, interest rate, employment), thereby ignoring important societal goals such as protection of nature, health, or social cohesion	*System goals* are pluralistic and socio-ecological in nature, using tokens as a multi-dimensional information signal and money substitute to promote positive action to benefit society at large [39, 70, 71]
System structure, consisting of governments, central banks, international financial organizations is hierarchical and only partly democratically legitimized	*System structure* is peer-to-peer, consisting of markets for positive action and dynamic governing bodies that are participatory and decentralized
System rules are defined top-down by the institutional structure through fiscal and monetary policy on national and international level	*System rules* for positive actions, token markets and governing bodies are self-organized and democratically governed with all users being able to participate

- The system encourages the bottom-up creation of token designs and their use via a permissionless, distributed peer-to-peer network.
- The governance of the system is democratic and decentralized to ensure division of power and continuous design for value.

Finance 4.0 is a new kind of monetary system, which makes systemic interventions more effective [72]. By considering different *goals*, Finance 4.0 can adapt its function over time and as required. By enabling *self-organization* at all levels, users hold the power to change the system, and let it evolve according to needs. Through the underlying *rules* of the cryptoeconomic system, incentives, punishments, and constraints can be co-designed [73]. They will co-evolve under the control of the users.

In summary, the new paradigm of the Finance 4.0 system opens new pathways that the current monetary system does not offer. It allows for monetary innovation by 'in-vitro' experiments exploring the post-fiat-monetary design space. I hope communities around the world will benefit from this chapter by finding and choosing, creating, and nurturing a prosperous economic system that respects their socio-ecological goals.

References

1. Y.N. Harari, *Sapiens: A Brief History of Humankind* (Signal Books, 2014)
2. N.G. Mankiw, *Principles of Economics*, 7th edn. (Cengage Learning, Stamford, CT, 2015)
3. Aristotle, *Nicomachean Ethics, Book 5, Chapter 5*, http://www.perseus.tufts.edu/hopper/text?doc=Perseus:text:1999.01.0054:book=5:chapter=5&highlight=shoemaker
4. J.G. Hülsmann, *The Ethics of Money Production* (Ludwig von Mises Inst, Auburn, Ala, 2008)
5. Aristotle, *Politics, Book 1, Section 1257a*, http://www.perseus.tufts.edu/hopper/text?doc=urn:cts:greekLit:tlg0086.tlg035.perseus-eng1:1.1257a
6. NPR, *Why Gold? A Chemist Explains Why Gold Beat Out Other Elements*, in *Planet Money, Morning Edition* (NPR, 2011)
7. H. Hazlitt, *What You Should Know About Inflation*, 2nd edn. (D. van Nostrand, New York, 1965)
8. S. Ammous, *The Bitcoin Standard: The Decentralized Alternative to Central Banking* (Wiley, Hoboken, New Jersey, 2018)
9. D. Lee (ed.), *Handbook of Digital Currency: Bitcoin, Innovation, Financial Instruments, and Big Data* (Elsevier/ AP, Amsterdam, 2015)
10. B.A. Lietaer, J. Dunne, *Rethinking Money: How New Currencies Turn Scarcity into Prosperity* (Berrett-Koehler Publishers, San Francisco, 2013)
11. R.E. Parker, R. Whaples (eds.), *Routledge Handbook of Major Events in Economic History* (Routledge, London; New York, 2013)
12. J.M. Keynes, *The General Theory of Employment, Interest and Money*, Vol. VII (Cambridge University Press for the Royal Economic Society, Cambridge [England] ; New York, 2013)
13. E.W. Kemmerer, *Gold and the Gold Standard: The Story of Gold Money, Past, Present and Future*, 1st edn. (McGraw-Hill, New York, 1944)
14. R.S. McElvaine (ed.), *Encyclopedia of the Great Depression* (Macmillan Reference USA, New York, 2004)
15. United States. Congress, *Gold Reserve Act of 1934* (1934)

16. Federal Reserve History, *Creation of the Bretton Woods System*, https://www.federalreserveh istory.org/essays/bretton_woods_created
17. P. Salin, *The International Monetary System and the Theory of Monetary Systems* (Edward Elgar Publishing, 2016)
18. P.-O. Gourinchas, H. Rey, M. Sauzet, *The International Monetary and Financial System*, Working Paper No. 25782, National Bureau of Economic Research, 2019
19. B. Bernanke, *Interview on CBS "60 Minutes"*, https://www.youtube.com/watch?v=hiCs_Y HlKSI
20. Deutsche Bundesbank, *Monatsbericht November 2020*, **72**, 164 (2020)
21. M. McLeay, A. Radia, R. Thomas, Money Creation in the Modern Economy. Bank of England Quarterly Bulletin **2014**, 14 (2014)
22. Basel Committee on Banking Supervision, Basel III Monitoring Report, Bank of International Settlements, 2020
23. S. Ugolini, *The Evolution of Central Banking: Theory and History* (Palgrave Macmillan, London, 2017)
24. F. Hutchinson, M. Mellor, W.K. Olsen, *The Politics of Money: Towards Sustainability and Economic Democracy* (Pluto, London ; Sterling, Va, 2002)
25. R. Dalio, *Principles for Navigating Big Debt Crises* (Greenleaf Book Group, Austin, 2018)
26. N. Irwin, *Of Kiwis and Currencies: How a 2% Inflation Target Became Global Economic Gospel*, (The New York Times, 2014)
27. Kristalina Georgieva (Managing Director IMF), *The Long Ascent: Overcoming the Crisis and Building a More Resilient Economy*, https://www.imf.org/en/News/Articles/2020/10/06/sp1 00620-the-long-ascent-overcoming-the-crisis-and-building-a-more-resilient-economy
28. D. Helbing, *Social Self-Organization: Agent-Based Simulations and Experiments to Study Emergent Social Behavior* (Springer, Berlin, 2012)
29. D. Andrews, F. Petroulakis, Breaking the Shackles: Zombie Firms, Weak Banks and Depressed Restructuring in Europe., No. 2240, European Central Bank, 2019
30. Bloomberg, *America's Zombie Companies Have Racked Up $1.4 Trillion of Debt*, Bloomberg.Com (2020)
31. C.M. Reinhart, K.S. Rogoff, *This Time Is Different: Eight Centuries of Financial Folly* (Princeton University Press, Princeton, 2009)
32. P. Bagus, *In Defense of Deflation* (Springer International Publishing, Cham, 2015)
33. F.P. Mongelli, D. Gerdesmeier, B. Roffia, *The Fed, the Eurosystem, and the Bank of Japan: More Similarities or Differences?*, https://voxeu.org/article/fed-eurosystem-and-bank-japan-similarities-and-differences
34. Board of Governors of the Federal Reserve System, The Federal Reserve System : Purposes and Functions, Board of Governors of the Federal Reserve System (U.S.), 2016
35. European Central Bank, *ECB Monetary Policy*, https://www.ecb.europa.eu/mopo/html/index. en.html
36. UN General Assembly, *Transforming Our World: The 2030 Agenda for Sustainable Development*, Division for Sustainable Development Goals: New York, NY, USA (2015)
37. K. Mainzer, *Thinking in Complexity: The Computational Dynamics of Matter, Mind, and Mankind*, 5th rev. and enl. ed (Springer, Berlin ; New York, 2007)
38. K. Raworth, *Doughnut Economics: Seven Ways to Think Like a 21st-Century Economist* (Random House Business, London, 2018)
39. K.-K. Kleineberg, D. Helbing, A "social bitcoin" could sustain a democratic digital world. Eur. Phys. J. Spec. Top. **225**, 3231 (2016), reprinted in this volume
40. G. Dosi A. Roventini, More is different… and complex! The case for agent-based macroeconomics. J Evol Econ **29**, 1 (2019)
41. D. Helbing, A. Kirman, Rethinking economics using complexity theory. Real-World Econ. Rev. **64**, 23–51 (2013) http://www.paecon.net/PAEReview/issue64/HelbingKirman64.pdf
42. P. Ormerod, D. Helbing, Back to the drawing board for macroeconomics. Chap. 18 in D. Cole (ed) *What's the Use of Economics?* (London Publishing Partnership, 2012), pp 131–151

43. C. Felber, *This Is Not Economy: Aufruf Zur Revolution Der Wirtschaftswissenschaft* (Paul Zsolnay Verlag, 2019)
44. P. Inman, *Economics Students Call for Shakeup of the Way Their Subject Is Taught*, The Guardian (2014)
45. F. Carapella, J. Flemming, Board of Governors of the Federal Reserve System, *Central Bank Digital Currency: A Literature Review*, FEDS Notes **2020**, (2020)
46. B. Cœuré, J. Loh, Central Bank Digital Currencies, Bank for International Settlements (2018)
47. Governing Council of the European Central Bank, Report on a Digital Euro, European Central Bank (2020)
48. Group of Thirty, *Digital Currencies and Stablecoins: Risks, Opportunities, and Challenges Ahead* (2020)
49. IMF, Digital Money Across Borders: Macro-Financial Implications, International Monetary Fund (2020)
50. S. Zuboff, *The age of surveillance capitalism: the fight for a human future at the new frontier of power*, 1st edn. (PublicAffairs, New York, 2019)
51. K.S. Rogoff, *The curse of cash* (Princeton University Press, Princeton, 2016)
52. S. Nakamoto, *Bitcoin: A Peer-to-Peer Electronic Cash System*, https://bitcoin.org/bitcoin.pdf
53. IMF, *World Economic Outlook Database: Report for Selected Countries and Subjects*, https://www.imf.org/en/Publications/WEO/weo-database/2020/October/weo-report
54. M. Friedrich, M. Weik, *Der größte Crash aller Zeiten: Wirtschaft, Politik, Gesellschaft : wie Sie jetzt noch Ihr Geld schützen können* (Eichborn, 2019)
55. N. Szabo, *Shelling Out: The Origins of Money*, https://nakamotoinstitute.org/shelling-out/
56. PlanB, *Modeling Bitcoin Value with Scarcity*, https://www.planBTC.com
57. P. Vigna, M.J. Casey, *The Age of Cryptocurrency: How Bitcoin and Digital Money Are Challenging the Global Economic Order* (St. Martin's Press, 2015)
58. F.A. Hayek, *Denationalisation of Money—The Argument Refined* (Ludwig von Mises Institute, 1990)
59. J.F. Nash, Ideal money. South. Econ. J. **69**, 4 (2002)
60. B.H. Bratton, *The stack: on software and sovereignty* (MIT press, Boston, 2016)
61. W. Bickel, D. Christensen (eds) *Behavioral Economics*, in *Encyclopedia of Psychopharmacology* (Springer Berlin Heidelberg, Berlin, Heidelberg, 2015), pp 259–263
62. N. Beckstead, On the Overwhelming Importance of Shaping the Far Future, Dissertation, State University of New Jersey (2013)
63. M. Fare, P.O. Ahmed, *Why Are Complementary Currency Systems Difficult to Grasp within Conventional Economics?*, Revue Interventions Économiques. Papers in Political Economy (2018)
64. A.E. Kazdin, *The Token Economy* (Springer, US, Boston, MA, 1977)
65. R.H. Thaler, C.R. Sunstein, *Nudge: improving decisions about health, wealth, and happiness* (Yale University Press, New Haven, 2008)
66. R.H. Thaler, Behavioral economics: past, present, and future. Am. Econ. Rev. **106**, 1577 (2016)
67. C. Vlek, L. Steg, Human behavior and environmental sustainability: problems, driving forces, and research topics. J. Soc. Issues **63**, 1 (2007)
68. E. Ostrom, *Governing the Commons: The Evolution of Institutions for Collective Action* (Cambridge University Press, Cambridge; New York, 1990)
69. S. Voshmgir, M. Zargham, Foundations of Cryptoeconomic Systems, No. 1, Vienna University of Economics (2019)
70. B. Kewell, R. Adams, G. Parry, Blockchain for good? Strateg Chang **26**, 429 (2017)
71. C. Dierksmeier, P. Seele, Cryptocurrencies and business ethics. J. Bus. Ethics **152**, 1 (2018)
72. D.H. Meadows, D. Wright, *Thinking in Systems: A Primer* (London [u.a.]: Earthscan, 2009
73. M.C. Ballandies, M.M. Dapp, E. Pournaras, Decrypting distributed ledger design—taxonomy, classification and blockchain community evaluation. Cluster Comput. (2021). https://doi.org/10.1007/s10586-021-03256-w

Qualified Money—A Better Financial System for the Future

Dirk Helbing

Abstract *Over millennia, people have seen the financial system collapse again and again. It is, therefore, time to re-invent money and the financial system altogether in order to make them fit for the complex world of today. Here, it is described how the idea for a new socio-ecological finance system came about. Three main innovations are proposed: (1) a particular combination of cash and electronic money, which promotes electronic transactions, while preserving privacy, where it is justified and needed; (2) money that has additional qualifiers such as reputation, which may depend on the geographic region, the exchange history, or other variables; (3) multidimensional money, which is better suited to manage complex systems such as our economy, and enables (the design of) self-organizing systems with favorable properties, e.g., economic systems that promote a co-evolutionary processes toward a circular economy.*

From Money to Bitcoin and Beyond

To discuss the future of money, let us look back a little bit. By inventing a universally interchangeable good, the historical invention of money made the exchange of goods much easier. But while money was based on valuable materials such as gold in the beginning, it was later increasingly replaced by symbolic values, such as paper bills, or even entries in a digital account. Now, money is created in great amounts not only by central banks. Normal banks do it as well. If, one day, we don't trust anymore that we will get valuable goods in exchange, it is obvious that the value of money

---

This chapter describes how the Finance 4.0 idea (also abbreviated by FIN4, FIN4+, or FIN+) was born. A preprint of this slightly edited chapter is available here: https://futurict.blogspot.com/2014/10/qualified-money-better-financial-system.html and https://papers.ssrn.com/sol3/papers.cfm?abstract_id=2526022.

D. Helbing (✉)
ETH Zurich, Computational Social Science, Stampfenbachstrasse 48, 8092 Zurich, Switzerland
e-mail: dhelbing@ethz.ch

© The Author(s) 2021   27
M. M. Dapp et al. (eds.), *Finance 4.0—Towards a Socio-Ecological Finance System*,
SpringerBriefs in Applied Sciences and Technology,
https://doi.org/10.1007/978-3-030-71400-0_2

will be gone. This process is known as "hyper-inflation." In human history, this has happened many times.

Bitcoin is an attempt to avoid that such a horrible scenario can happen again. It's a peer-to-peer payment system, which does not require banks anymore. But it has other problems. Bitcoins are designed such that the overall amount of digital currency is slowly growing and saturating, thereby establishing something like a new "gold standard." However, in history, a classical gold standard alone has not been flexible enough for a resilient financial system.[1] If the volume of money grows more quickly than economic output, there will eventually be inflation. Then, the value of money, i.e., its purchasing power, will drop. Conversely, if the volume of money does not grow as quickly as productivity, one may run into another problem, called "deflation." Then, money becomes more valuable over time, and people would hoard rather than spend it, as they can buy goods more cheaply in the future. Under such conditions, business cannot thrive. So, the volume of money should grow proportional to productivity, at least on average. Let me add though that the above dependencies regarding inflation and deflation are expected to hold only on the long run. Central banks and other stakeholders can manipulate financial markets, which may create delayed adjustments, biases, and abnormal market behaviors. As a consequence, it becomes increasingly difficult to interpret market signals correctly and to respond to them in a proper way. On the long run, I think, loss of control is almost inevitable.

A New Kind of Money: How the Idea Was Born

For the above reasons and due to the large amount of energy consumed, Bitcoin will not be the final solution, but the technological concept that is behind it will probably guide the way for future currencies and other services requiring secure transactions. Altogether, however, we need to fundamentally re-invent money, it is not adaptive enough for our complex world. We have to ask ourselves, why the financial system keeps crashing since thousands of years, and what is fundamentally wrong with the way we have set it up.

Thinking about this for a couple of years, I came to the conclusion that even though money is a great invention, it's outdated. Therefore, it's time to create a better one. The argument is as follows: Currently, money is a scalar, i.e., the simplest mathematical quantity one can think of. It is neither multi-dimensional nor does it have a memory. But mathematics offers a much richer spectrum of concepts to define exchange processes, such as multi-dimensional quantities, e.g., vectors,

---

[1]To make the gold standard more flexible, one could create gold-backed digital money with a time stamp. This would allow one to introduce "artificial aging" of money. In other words, such money would be most valuable when handed out, but it would lose its value exponentially over time. However, the same amount of money that would be lost in this way would be newly generated, for example, for the payment of basic income and investment premiums, see https://www. springerprofessional.de/democratic-capitalism/18842560 or http://futurict.blogspot.com/2020/07/democratic-capitalism-why-not-give-it.html.

tensors, matrices, or network graphs. In fact, money comes from somewhere and goes somewhere else. Who transfers money to whom defines a network of money flows. Therefore, money should be represented by network quantities. And money should be multi-dimensional to allow other things to happen apart from the eternal ups and downs.

This made me think about "Qualified Money"—multi-dimensional money with a memory. Since Roman times, people have said: "Money doesn't stink!" In other words, it does not matter where it comes from and how it is earned. However, what if we could give it a scent, like a perfume? And what if this would co-determine the value of money? In a discussion during a visit in Zurich, my colleagues Tobias Preis, David Rand, and Ole Peters were fascinated by this idea. Later on, I combined it with a reputation system and called the new concept "Qualified Money." Such money could earn reputation and, with this, additional value! This approach has commonalities with local currencies, but it is more general and relates to the way, modern stock markets work. However, Qualified Money opens entirely new possibilities.

What's Wrong with Our Financial Architecture?

One of the problems of today's financial system is the possibility of cascading effects. What started as a local problem in the Californian real estate market became a world financial and economic crisis, eventually causing social and political unrests. But how could it come that far? For this, see the Fig. 1 below. The world financial system lacks engineered breaking points to stop cascades. At home, every one of us has electrical fuses to make sure that a local electrical overload would not cause a larger problem, e.g., the house to burn down. In the financial system, however, the strategy is just the opposite: to ease the load on troubled banks, some of their problems have been taken on by the states, which are now in trouble as well, and so on. Rather than isolating infected "patients" and curing them by an intensive care program, one infected many other countries that were healthy before. In this way, the overall damage became much larger than it could have been, and it is not clear how we will ever recover from the resulting debt levels. If we don't get the problems solved any time soon, cultural values such as tolerance and solidarity, or even peace might be in danger. It's now the very fabric of our society, which is at stake. In societies with mass unemployment, it can take two generations or more until the good relationships between citizens and their state and a healthy social structure recovers.

What worries even more is the fact that we don't currently have a backup financial system. For most other systems that may fail, we have contingency plans—a "plan B" or "plan C." In fact, one might argue that one reason why our current financial system performs badly is the absence of competing financial systems. Given that we believe in competition, why don't we take this seriously and build alternative systems, which could also serve as backups, as plans B or C? It's not enough to complain about having to bail out banks and about lacking alternatives. I also doubt that tougher regulations won't fix the problems. As large banks can handle the additional

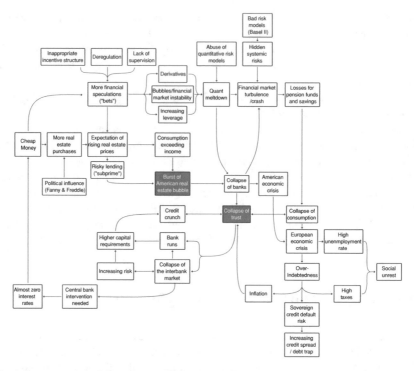

Fig. 1 How cascading effects in financial markets can come about

regulations best, while small- and medium-sized banks struggle with them, these regulations may cause big banks to grow even bigger. Therefore, we should rather promote alternatives. In fact, with Bitcoin and peer-to-peer lending systems, some alternatives are eventually emerging, but we need more and better ones.

At the moment, I would say that we cannot take it for granted that the current financial system will still work in 10 or 20 years from now. Most industrial states have debts of the order of 100% of the gross domestic product (GDP), sometimes even a multiple of this. Controlled inflation has been considered to be a recipe to reduce these debts. The trick can work, if applied by a single country or just a few ones. However, if the USA, Europe, China, Japan, and further countries are all trying to reduce their debts in such a way at the same time, this may trigger an inflationary spiral that can get out of hand.

Besides, the attempts of central banks to control the level of inflation haven't worked well so far. To save banks, to encourage investments into the real economy, and to increase the level of inflation, central banks have pumped massive, almost unimaginable amounts of money into the financial markets (under labels such as "quantitative easing"). However, as it turns out, years after the financial crisis started, many problems have still not been sorted out.

Why is this? Banks often do not trust that companies would pay their loans back and, besides, they need more capitalization themselves. Most money created by the central banks does not reach the companies in need. Instead, given the low interest rates, money is mainly invested in financial markets. This drives up stock prices even when real economic growth is negligible or negative. Rising stock prices create further incentives for virtual investments at the stock markets rather than real investments into companies. Consequently, central banks have created a gigantic bubble in the financial markets. In some sense, a virtual inflation has happened over there—the stocks have become more expensive even though most companies haven't grown. When this stock market bubble bursts, a large fraction of the money will flee into real values. This will suddenly drive enormous price inflation, as there are not enough material values that these huge amounts of money can buy. Therefore, inflation might easily get out of control. So far, this did not happen, as misleading incentives have caused a temporary allocation of money in the stock markets. In the meantime, however, low interest rates are undermining the perspectives of life insurances and pension funds.

An Unfeasible Control Problem

I have argued above that the central banks haven't been able to reach the effects they wanted. But this is not because they wouldn't be competent. It's because the control problem they are faced with is ill-defined—it's literally unsolvable. The reason is that they don't have enough instruments or, to put it differently, not enough control variables. The central banks can increase the volume of money, and they can change the interest rate. That's basically it. They may also buy and sell bonds, but many think they shouldn't. The classical instruments of central banks are apparently not sufficient to do the job. In other words, the weapons of central banks are blunt. New possibilities are urgently needed, and this basically means additional ways of adaptation.

Why is this so? Let's take an example from the world of taxes. Apart from raising money for public investments, taxes are often used to incentivize or discourage certain kinds of behaviors. For example, many countries have taxes on cigarettes, alcohol, and fuel, to reduce their consumption. They may also offer tax reductions for investments into environmental-friendly heating, better home insulation, or buying solar panels, to promote the production of renewable energy. It is clear that each of these goals can be achieved by suitable taxation-based incentives. But what happens if one simultaneously tries to reach many goals by one single "control variable," the overall amount of money to be paid for taxes? One may end up investing into solar energy production, while smoking more cigarettes, which altogether would not change the individual tax level. So, on average, people may not be very responsive to a multitude of rewards and sanctions. In other words, we are unlikely to reach many goals with a single control variable such as one-dimensional money.

More "Control Variables" Needed

This problem is actually well-known from control theory. For example, complex chemical production processes cannot be steered by a single control variable such as the temperature or the concentration of a certain chemical ingredient. In a complicated production process, one must be able to control many different variables, such as the pressure and the concentrations of all ingredients. It is also instructive to compare this with ecosystems. The plant and animal life in a place will not just be determined by a single control variable such as the amount of water, but also by the temperature, humidity, and various kinds of nutrients such as oxygen, nitrogen, and phosphor. Our bodies, too, require many kinds of vitamins and nutrients to be healthy. So, why should our economic system be different? Why shouldn't a healthy financial system need several kinds of money?

If we had different kinds of money, we could probably influence how much of the money handed out by central banks is finally used by companies for real investments. This would require at least one additional kind of money. So, let us assume that, besides cash and goods, we would have two kinds of electronic money: "real" electronic money ("REMO") and "virtual" electronic money ("VEM"). For example, besides real electronic EUROs, we could introduce "AEROs" as virtual electronic money. By law, cash and real electronic money could be invested into goods and real investments, but not into financial products. Virtual electronic money, in contrast, could be invested into financial products, but not into goods. The important point is now that the central bank could hand out REMO and VEM at different interest rates. If REMO were handed out at a lower interest rate than VEM, this would incentivize real investments.

Two Kinds of Electronic Money

Of course, cash, REMO and VEM could be converted into each other. However, by means of conversion fees, one could also create incentives for one kind of money as compared to the other(s). This would create new "degrees of freedom", as a physicist would say, which would enable a better adaptation of the financial system to the actual needs. For example, if REMO earns some interest rate but cash not, or if cash loses value due to inflation, this speaks against saving large amounts of cash. It would be better to spend cash on consumption, or to turn it into REMO or VEM. If lending REMO is cheaper than lending VEM, it will incentivize real investments over virtual investments into financial products. If VEM can be converted into REMO for free, but converting REMO into VEM is costly, this again incentivizes real investments.

So, this little extension of our financial system will allow the central banks to more effectively stimulate real investments into companies' production capacities. Central banks would not have to produce anymore a bubble of cheap money, which will sooner or later overheat the financial and real estate markets. As we have seen in the past, this can cause dangerously large bubbles, which will sooner or later produce large-scale global damage, when they burst.

Europe's "Little" Mistake

But we should dare to think one step further. While the economy in the USA and the UK seems to be recovering from the 2008 financial crash and the subsequent economic crisis, most of Europe is still not doing well after several years of struggle—in fact, some indicators are worse than after the great depression in the 1930s. In January 2014, Nobel Prize winner Joe Stiglitz (*1943) summarized the situation in Basel, Switzerland, as follows: before the crisis, Europe was doing very well. It had some of the strongest economies in the world, it had some of the best public infrastructures, best education systems, best health systems, and social systems. However, Europe did a "little" mistake: without creating a sufficiently sophisticated institutional framework, it introduced a new currency, the EURO, which replaced more than a dozen other currencies. Altogether, this created more problems than benefits, he judged.

We are not talking here about the widespread complaint of citizens that the introduction of the EURO made life more expensive—be it justified or not. Instead, we must talk about the fact that, if we compare all countries on a one-dimensional scale such as the gross domestic product (GDP) per capita, there will be always winners and losers. In this case, Germany happens to be a winner and Greece a loser, but it could have been different as well. We must recognize that, given the different productivity of the countries, it was just a matter of time until economic forces were unleashed, which required adjustments. In the past, such adjustments happened naturally by adapting the currency exchange rates. Now, in more than 15 European countries, this is not possible anymore. This problem can again be solved by adding new "degrees of freedom", or, as other people say, new "control variables". But how to introduce these variables without giving up the EURO, which many consider an important peace-building project in Europe?

Vitamins for the Financial System

In the following, I will suggest to introduce "Qualified Money." Qualified Money has a number of different qualifiers, which turn money into a multi-dimensional means of exchange. The value of Qualified Money is not only given by its amount, but also a conversion factor that depends on various qualities. For example, if one decided that geographic origin should be a qualifier, one would enable country-specific EUROs, allowing adjustments of the value of money to the respective economic strength. The same approach can be used to define regional or local currencies, if desired. So, one could save the prestige project of the "EURO" by making the currency more flexible.

The regional variants of EUROs would be converted into each other similarly as we are currently doing it for different kinds of currencies at the stock markets, such as EUROs, DOLLARs, or YENs.

However, Qualified Money would not *have* to be connected to local origin. The concept has potential for extension. For example, the unemployment rate, the Millennium development goals, or any socio-economic-environmental factors considered relevant for human well-being could be used to define qualifiers. In our lives, it's not just money that matters. People care about many things, and this opens up entirely new possibilities!

We Could All Be Doing Well

It is important to recognize that both, the self-organization and management of complex dynamical systems, require sufficiently many control variables, not just one. Establishing different kinds of money would serve this purpose. Compared to the currency system we have today, these different kinds of money would not be easily convertible. There would be an adjustable conversion tax or fee, to discourage conversion and to encourage earning different kinds of money, instead. This would naturally extend the approach we have discussed before (in connection with VEM and REMO), and it would create a multi-dimensional incentive system, rewarding us for different kinds of efforts, including social and environmental ones.

Of course, such a conversion tax or fee would create something like "friction" in the multi-dimensional money system. However, we know from physics that friction can enable important functionality. How would it be to have such a multi-dimensional money and exchange system? Depending on how many dimensions we allow for, everyone could be doing well, each one on the dimensions fitting his or her personal strengths, skills, or expertise.

Today, we have many ranking systems to compensate for the lack of such a multi-dimensional money system. Besides the Fortune 500 list of richest persons, we rank tennis players and soccer players. Others collect medals or decorations, or even scores in computer games. Scientists enjoy citations earned by publications... Even though some of these ranking scales don't imply any material value, they can motivate people to make an effort. Hence, we can use such incentive mechanisms to create a multi-dimensional reward system, as we need it to enable self-organizing socio-economic systems.

One might even consider the possibility to allow everyone to establish a certain number of own currencies. In a sense, this would be the logical next step after allowing banks and Bitcoin (not just central banks) to create money. The value of these personalized currencies would then depend on how much others trust in them and are willing to engage in related value exchanges. I assume that, after some time, there would be just a reasonably small number of successful currencies that are widely used. However, they might have some interesting new properties compared to the currencies we have today. Therefore, opening up money creation to innovation might be really worthwhile.

Money with a Memory

Let us now assume that electronic money would be traceable. In this case, we could give electronic money a "memory," and we could make its value dependent on its transaction history. To put it in simple terms, money that went through the hands of Albert Einstein or John F. Kennedy could have more value than money that was earned with "blood diamonds." So, possible qualifiers could be, how the money was earned, its origin or destination location, the reputation of the products bought, or the reputation of the producer or seller. Hence, we can further differentiate electronic money by means of additional qualifiers. This might be imagined as treating money units like stocks or like individual currencies. In other words, a (reputation-dependent) conversion factor would apply, when financial transactions are made.

Benefits of Money with Reputation

I recognize that some people might feel uneasy about money becoming dependent on reputation. However, in some sense, this is already happening when we go shopping on the Internet. Depending on the country we live in, the type of computer we are using, and perhaps further personal qualifiers such as income, we might get different product offers than others, at different prices. This is part of the logic of personalized recommender systems. One might find it upsetting to pay a higher price than others, but it could also be a lower one. When we book an airplane ticket or a hotel room, we receive different offers, too, depending on when we book and where we book, and whether we are regular customers or not.

In any case, there are quite some benefits of reputation-based Qualified Money. For example, it becomes easier for producers and stores to sell high-quality products at a higher price. Furthermore, to get an idea how future shopping might look like, assume that there is a database, in which information about products is stored, such as the amount of money to be paid, ingredients, durability, level of environmental-friendly production, level of socially friendly production, and much more. In addition, let's assume our smartphones know our preferences, for example, that we give the price a weight of 50%, environmental-friendliness a weight of 30%, and fair production a weight of 20%, and that we want to avoid products with particular ingredients we are allergic against. Then, by scanning product codes and retrieving the related product information, our smartphone will recommend us the best fitting products.[2]

---

[2]Such a platform for more sustainable consumption has been presented in a recent publication: T. Asikis, J. Klinglmayr, D. Helbing and E. Pournaras, How value-sensitive design can empower

Furthermore, if customers were willing to share their preference settings, producers and sellers could better tailor their assortment of products to the customer wishes. Therefore, customers would benefit as well. They would get more products they would really like to have.

Balancing Transparency and Anonymity

If properly set up, Qualified Money can create a good balance between transparency and anonymity, such that we can have the benefits of both. Transparency can promote more responsible and desirable behavior. It allows ethical values and higher quality to survive in a framework of free economic competition. In fact, a considerable fraction of people cares about ethics and fair products. Even financial investors are getting interested in ethical investments, as they tend to be more sustainable. At the moment, we often find ourselves in a situation, where the competition between companies is so harsh that they have to reduce production costs. This can sooner or later decrease salary levels, production standards, product quality, and/or sustainability. In the end, we may have lower salary levels or lower-quality products. Both will eventually impact producers as well. In contrast, reputation mechanisms could stop the undesirable downward spiral, by rewarding higher quality products and fairer production.

The question is, whether the transparency needed for such reputation systems will ever be reached? In fact, there is currently a trend toward more transparency of money flows. We have recently seen (some of) the Swiss banking secrecy melt away. Several times, whistleblowers have sold confidential information about private accounts to public authorities. "Off-Shore Leaks" has made international money flows more transparent as well. Furthermore, there seems to be a "follow the money" program that tracks individual money transactions. And presently, many countries set up agreements for an automatic information exchange allowing public authorities to monitor money flows and to check tax declarations.

Anonymous money exchange is under attack for similar reasons as anonymous information exchange: In many cases, it has promoted crime and misery. Nevertheless, anonymity has still important roles to play. Most of us don't want others to know, what medicine we buy in a pharmacy. For such and further reasons, we should still have some amount of cash besides traceable electronic money, even though it should lose its value quickly enough to make traceable transactions more attractive than cash.

It should be also remembered that anonymity is one of the most important elements of democracies. The principle of anonymous vote is needed for independent decision-making, which is a precondition for the "wisdom of crowds" to

sustainable consumption, Royal Society Open Science 8: 201418 (2021); see also the video accessible at https://www.youtube.com/watch?v=uur5BXXspgI.

work. Academic peer review as well is based on anonymity, to support open criticism without fear of revenge. Organized crime or corruption would also be difficult to fight without protecting the anonymity of witnesses. So, neither full transparency nor full anonymity can work. We need a system that makes it possible to combine and balance both principles. Introducing Qualified Money besides cash is the solution!

How this would work is described in more detail in an invention,[3] a FuturICT blog on Democratic Capitalism,[4] as well as the main part of this book on "Finance 4.0" and its Appendix on the "Interaction Support Processor".

---

[3]D. Helbing, Interaction Support Processor, see https://patents.google.com/patent/US2016035068 5A1/en.

[4]See http://futurict.blogspot.com/2020/07/democratic-capitalism-why-not-give-it.html, to be published in D. Helbing, Next Civilization (Springer, 2021).

A "Social Bitcoin" Could Sustain a Democratic Digital World

Kaj-Kolja Kleineberg and Dirk Helbing

Abstract *A multidimensional financial system could provide benefits for individuals, companies, and states. Instead of top-down control, which is destined to eventually fail in a hyperconnected world, a bottom-up creation of value can unleash creative potential and drive innovations. Multiple currency dimensions can represent different externalities and thus enable the design of incentives and feedback mechanisms that foster the ability of complex dynamical systems to self-organize and lead to a more resilient society and sustainable economy. Modern information and communication technologies play a crucial role in this process, as Web 2.0 and online social networks promote cooperation and collaboration on unprecedented scales. Within this contribution, we discuss how one dimension of a multidimensional currency system could represent socio-digital capital (Social Bitcoins) that can be generated in a bottom-up way by individuals who perform search and navigation tasks in a future version of the digital world. The incentive to mine Social Bitcoins could sustain digital diversity, which mitigates the risk of totalitarian control by powerful monopolies of information and can create new business opportunities needed in times where a large fraction of current jobs is estimated to disappear due to computerization.*

Modern Socio-Economic Challenges Require a New Approach

Nowadays, we are facing a number of serious problems such as financial instabilities, an unsustainable economy and related global warming, the lack of social cooperation and collaboration causing the rise of conflict, terrorism and war. Traditional

This chapter was first published by Springer as an article in *The European Physical Journal Special Topics* 225, 3231–3241 (2016) under the same title.

K.-K. Kleineberg (✉) · D. Helbing
ETH Zurich, Computational Social Science, Stampfenbachstrasse 48, 8092 Zurich, Switzerland
e-mail: kajkoljakleineberg@gmail.com

© The Author(s) 2021   39
M. M. Dapp et al. (eds.), *Finance 4.0—Towards a Socio-Ecological Finance System*,
SpringerBriefs in Applied Sciences and Technology,
https://doi.org/10.1007/978-3-030-71400-0_3

approaches to remedy such problems are based on top-down control. Whereas in the past this way of thinking worked reasonably well, the high interconnectivity in modern systems will eventually but unavoidably lead to its failure as systems become uncontrollable by central entities due to stronger internal effects, leading to often unpredictable cascading behavior [1] and catastrophic failures [2].

Instead of entirely top-down-based approaches, designing mechanisms to promote desired results like increased cooperation, coordination, and better resource efficiency could help to deal with current socio-economic challenges. Importantly, a multidimensional incentive system is needed to design the desired interactions and appropriate feedback mechanisms [3, 4]. Such incentives have to be implemented in a bottom-up way, allowing systems to self-organize [5] and thus promoting creativity, innovation, and diversity [6].

Diversity acts as a motor of innovation, can promote collective intelligence [7], and is fundamental for the resilience of society [8, 9]. This renders socio-economic and cultural diversity equally important as biodiversity. The importance of diversity, however, is not restricted to individual, cultural, social, or economic domains. For instance, diversity among digital services in competition for the attention of users can mitigate the risk of totalitarian control and manipulation by extremely powerful monopolies of information. As we explain in Sect. 3.3, the loss of diversity in the digital world can lead to a systematic and irreversible collapse of the digital ecosystem [10, 11], akin to the loss of biodiversity in the physical ecosystem. Such a collapse can have dramatic consequences for the freedom of information and eventually for the freedom of society. In this contribution, we show how such a catastrophic collapse could be avoided on a systematic level by introducing a multidimensional incentive system in which an appropriately designed cryptocurrency provides an incentive for individuals to perform certain tasks in their socio-digital environment. We refer to this cryptocurrency as "Social Bitcoins." [1]

Importantly, to successfully meet these challenges, tools, ideas, and concepts from complexity science have to be combined with technologies like the blockchain, economic knowledge (and potentially Internet of Things technology to measure "externalities").

A Multidimensional Financial System

The invention of money has led to unprecedented wealth and has provided countless benefits for society. However, the current monetary system is not appropriate any more to control highly interconnected dynamical complex systems like the ones our economy and financial system nowadays form. Whereas such systems are in general difficult to control and understand and nearly impossible to predict, they exhibit the

---

[1] The details of the implementation of such a cryptocurrency are beyond the scope of this contribution.

tendency to self-organize [5, 12]. New approaches to face today's challenges should therefore take advantage of this system intrinsic tendency.

Central banks like the ECB can control the amount of money in the market by means ranging from adjusting interest rates to quantitative easing. Recently, the ECB has lowered interest rates to the lowest value of all time (even introducing negative rates for some bank deposits [13]) and has further increased its efforts to buy government bonds [14]. These measures are intended to boost economy and increase inflation in the Euro zone to the target of 2%. Despite these efforts, inflation has remained close to 0%, raising doubts about the capacity to act and the credibility of the ECB [15]. Furthermore, liquidity pumped into the market does not reach efficiently enough the real economy. As a consequence recently "helicopter money" has been discussed as a possible solution [16, 17]. Importantly, these problems are not limited to the Euro zone. For example, due to the interconnected nature of our economic and financial systems, the state of the global economy limits the decisions the Fed can take concerning a raise of interest rates, as such a raise could pose a threat for the global economy [18].

The problem is that the current monetary system provides only a one-dimensional control variable. Let us consider the human body and how it self-organizes as an example. To ensure its healthy function, it is not enough to adjust only the amount of water one drinks. Instead, the body needs water, air, carbohydrate, different proteins and vitamins, mineral nutrients, and more. None of these needs can be replaced by another. Why should this be different in systems like our economy, the financial system, or society?

Indeed, a multidimensional currency system could help to solve the problems mentioned above, where the different dimensions can be converted at a low (or negligible) cost. Such multidimensional incentive system could be used to promote self-organization of financial and economic systems in a bottom-up way [19]. This opens the door to "Capitalism 2.0" and "Finance 4.0" (see [20–23] for details).

A special case of a multidimensional incentive system is "qualified money." The concept was first introduced by Dirk Helbing in [19, 22]. Instead of a scalar (one-dimensional) quantity, like the Euro or any other currency, money could be multidimensional and earn its own reputation. To illustrate this, consider the example that there were two dimensions of money. By law, the first could only be invested into real values, but not into financial products. Instead, the latter dimension could. There would be an exchange rate (and cost) to convert one dimension into the other. As a consequence, the ECB could increase the amount of money for real investments directly, hence avoiding the problem mentioned earlier. In other words, the decision space on which institutions like the ECB can act would considerably increase without them acting outside of their mandate. Qualified money, which could be realized in a Bitcoin-like [24] way,[2] could earn its own reputation depending on how and where it was created and what businesses it supports. The reputation then can give the money

---

[2]That means, transactions are transparent. It is important to have a dimension of qualified money which cannot be tracked, and this dimension should lose value more rapidly to incentive spending it soon. See [22] for details.

more or less value, which can lead to a more sustainable economy as sustainability would become measurable and transparent to individuals (for details see [20, 22]). The concept of qualified money is not limited to the above-described two dimensions. Instead, everything people care about can be represented by a dimension in the currency vector. As we explain in the following, one dimension of qualified money could be socio-digital capital that can be acquired in the digital world.

Modern information and communication technologies play an important role in facing today's challenges. Indeed, nowadays the digital and physical world are strongly interdependent and cannot be treated in isolation any more [1]. The huge success of Web 2.0 and online social networks is changing the way humans interact at a global scale. They promote cooperation and collaboration on unprecedented scales, but at the same time powerful monopolies of information have the power to alter individuals' emotions and decisions [25, 26]. Supercomputers nowadays perform a large fraction of all financial transactions, hence influencing the prices of important commodities, which can lead to starving, conflicts, war, etc. Information and communication technologies thus are both a crucial part of the problems society has to solve as well as a fundamental and promising piece of the solution.

Decentralized Information Architectures and Qualified Money: A Social Bitcoin

Decentralized Architectures

The existence of powerful monopolies of information like big IT-companies or even some governments can lead to the loss of control by individuals, companies, or states. Besides, the economic damage attributed to cybercrime is growing exponentially and is estimated to reach 2.1 trillion dollars in 2019 [27]. Hence, it is time to design more resilient information and communication technologies that—by design—cannot be exploited by single entities. Decentralized architectures naturally provide these benefits [28–30].

Social Bitcoins and Web 4.0

As explained earlier, the main idea behind qualified money is to price a broader spectrum of externalities. This means that it can be applied to, for instance, information. This can be realized in many different ways. The exact details would probably emerge in a self-organized way, depending on choices and preferences of individuals. But how could such a system look like and what benefits would it provide? Here, we discuss a possible vision in which one dimension of qualified money, socio-digital capital, can be priced in terms of Social Bitcoins that can be mined using online social networks and digital infrastructures. It is impossible to foresee the exact details of such a system; nevertheless, in the following, we will sketch a possible vision of a future Internet and digital world in which individuals perform the routing of messages and information using their social contacts and technological connections rather than relying on service providers.

The use of the Internet has changed fundamentally since its invention. At first, it was a collection of static web pages. Then, Web 2.0 emerged as "a collaborative medium, a place where we [could] all meet and read and write" [31]. Consequently, Web 3.0 constitutes a "Semantic Web" [31], where data can be processed by machines. Let us refer to a digital world in which information is managed in a bottom-up way, free of central monopolies in control of the vast majority of information, as Web 4.0.[3] A digital democracy [28], if you will. Assume that this digital world was composed of many interacting, decentralized systems, which—in the absence of central control compete for the attention of individuals [10, 11]. As we explain in Sect. 3.3, such a state is possible but fragile. Now assume that, in the future of the Internet, each individual routes information using their social and technological connections rather than relying on service providers.[4] In decentralized architectures, this task has to be performed relying only on local knowledge. As shown in [33], this type of routing can be performed very efficiently and—most importantly—can be perfected if individuals actively use multiple networks simultaneously.[5] This fact constitutes an important starting point to design appropriate incentives to sustain digital democracy.

Assume that individuals could earn Social Bitcoins by routing information in the way explained above. These Social Bitcoins would form a dimension of qualified money [19, 20, 22] and could (with some additional cost) be exchanged and hence converted into other dimensions of the currency vector. Their exchange rate would depend on the trust individuals have in the system and how much they value their socio-digital environment.

The important point is that now individuals have an incentive to route information ("mining" Social Bitcoins). As a consequence, individuals will optimize to some extend their capabilities to perform this action. As explained above and shown in [33], the routing success can be increased and even perfected if individuals actively use many networks simultaneously.[6] Hence, the introduction of a Social Bitcoin would constitute an incentive to be active in several networks, as illustrated in Fig. 1. In addition, search and navigation tasks taking place in less active networks could increase the reputation of the mined Social Bitcoins, providing further incentive to engage in less active networks. In other words, sustainability in the digital world

---

[3]In [32] Web 4.0 is described as follows: "Web 4.0 will be as a read-write-execution concurrency web with intelligent interactions, but there is still no exact definition of it. Web 4.0 is also known as symbiotic web in which human mind and machines can interact in symbiosis."

[4]It is important to note that this new type of information routing requires efficient and secure encryption to ensure privacy of individuals, whenever they wish so.

[5]This is only the case if the different networks are related such that they exhibit *geometric correlations*. As shown in [33], real systems obey this condition.

[6]In addition, there are other aspects individuals might optimize, see for instance [34].

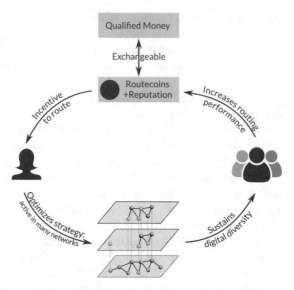

Fig. 1 Illustration of the incentive to mine Social Bitcoins. Social Bitcoins form one dimension of qualified money and can be mined by performing search and navigation tasks using social and technological connections in a future digital world. Hence, acquiring Social Bitcoins constitutes an incentive to perform routing. Individuals optimize their strategy to route information and will be active simultaneously in more networks, as this (among other aspects [34]) increases routing performance [33]. Performing routing in less active networks could increase the reputation of the mined Social Bitcoins, providing an additional incentive to engage in less active networks. This then could sustain digital diversity [10, 11] and at the same time increase the performance of routing

could be priced and would become transparent to individuals who then could adjust their behavior accordingly. Importantly, as we explain in detail in the following, this optimization could make digital diversity robust and sustainable.

How a Social Bitcoin Could Sustain Digital Diversity

Here, we present a mathematical model to illustrate the potential effect of a Social Bitcoin. As mentioned earlier, many digital services compete for the attention of individuals. In this context, the attention of users can be considered a scarce resource, and hence, the digital world forms a complex ecosystem in which networks represent competing species. A concise description of the digital ecology was developed in [10]. In a nutshell, multiple online social networks compete for the attention of individuals in addition to obeying their intrinsic evolutionary dynamics. This dynamics is given by two main mechanisms, the influence of mass media and a viral spreading dynamics acting on top of pre-existing underlying offline social networks [35]. Importantly, the parameter that quantifies the strength of viral spreading, λ, determines the final fate of the network. If λ is below a critical value λ_c, the network will eventually become entirely passive, which corresponds to the death of the network. On the other hand, for $\lambda > \lambda_c$, the activity of the network is sustained [35, 36]. The competition between multiple networks can be modeled assuming that more active networks are more attractive to users. Hence, the total virality, which reflects the overall involvement of individuals in online social networks, is distributed between the different networks as a function of their activities. More active networks obtain a higher share of the virality, which then makes these networks more active. Note that this induces a rich-get-richer effect. Interestingly, despite this positive feedback loop, diminishing returns induced by the network dynamics allows for a stable coexistence (digital diversity) of several networks in a certain parameter range (we refer the reader to [10] for details).

The system can be described by the following meanfield equations[7]

$$\dot{\rho}_i^a = \rho_i^a \left\{ \lambda \langle k \rangle \omega_i(\boldsymbol{\rho}^a)[1 - \rho_i^a] - 1 \right\}, \quad i = 1, \ldots, n, \tag{1}$$

where ρ_i^a denotes the fraction active users in network i, λ is the total virality mentioned earlier, and $\langle k \rangle$ denotes the mean degree of network, i.e., the average number of connections each node has. The weights $\omega_i(\boldsymbol{\rho}^a)$ depend on the activities in all networks, $\boldsymbol{\rho}^a = (\rho_1^a, \rho_2^a, \ldots, \rho_n^a)$, and govern the distribution of virality between different networks. In [10] the authors used $\omega_i(\boldsymbol{\rho}^a) = [\rho_i^a]^\sigma / \sum_{j=1}^n [\rho_j^a]^\sigma$, where σ denotes the activity affinity that quantifies how much more prone individuals are to engage in more active networks.

As mentioned earlier, assume that the introduction of Social Bitcoins incentivizes users to simultaneously use multiple networks in order to increase their capabilities to successfully perform search and navigation tasks and hence increase their expected payoff. The exact form of this incentive depends on the details of the implementation of the systems' architectures and Social Bitcoins, which comprises an interesting future research direction. Here, we model the additional tendency of individuals to engage in multiple (and less active) networks by shifting the weight of the distribution of the virality toward networks with lower activity, hence hindering the rich-get-richer effect described earlier. In particular, let us consider the following form of the weight function [10],

$$\omega_i(\boldsymbol{\rho}^a) = \underbrace{\frac{[\rho_i^a]^\sigma}{\sum_{j=1}^{n_l} [\rho_j^a]^\sigma}}_{\text{rich-get-richer [10]}} + \underbrace{\xi(\langle \boldsymbol{\rho}^a \rangle - \rho_i^a)}_{\text{Social Bitcoin incentive}}, \tag{2}$$

where ξ is a parameter proportional to the value of Social Bitcoins and $\langle \rho^a \rangle = \frac{1}{n} \sum_{i=1}^n \rho_i^a$ denotes the mean activity among all networks.

---

[7]In the framework of [10], these equations are the result of taking the limit of $\nu \to \infty$, where ν describes the ratio between the rate at which the viral spreading and the influence of mass media occur. As shown in [10], taking this limit has no impact on the stability of the system.

The effect of the inclusion of the new term ("Social Bitcoin incentive") in Eq. (2) can change the behavior of the system dramatically if ξ is large enough, which we illustrate[8] for two competing networks. Let us first consider the case of $\xi = 0.2$. In this case, the qualitative behavior of the system is similar to the one in absence of Social Bitcoins as described in [10]. Below a critical value of the activity affinity, $\sigma < \sigma_c$, coexistence is possible (solid green central branch in Fig. 2 (top) and central green diamond in Fig. 2 (middle, left)), but—once lost—cannot be recovered.

To illustrate this, assume that we start with $\sigma < \sigma_c$, and the system approaches the coexistence solution (central green diamond in Fig. 3 (middle, left)). Then, we change σ to some value larger than σ_c. Hence, the coexistence solution becomes unstable and the system eventually approaches the solution where either $\rho 1 = 0$ or $\rho 2 = 0$ (green diamonds in Fig. 2 (middle, right)). Now, after changing σ back to a value below σ_c, the system does not return to the again stable coexistence state, but instead remains in the domination state, which is also stable (outer green diamonds in Fig. 2 (middle, left)). This example is illustrated in Fig. 2 (bottom), where we explicitly show the evolution of the fraction of active users for both networks.[9] To conclude, the system is fragile in the sense that an irreversible loss of digital diversity is possible—similar to the loss of biodiversity.

Interestingly, for a higher value of ξ the behavior of the system differs dramatically, which we illustrate here for $\xi = 1$. The solution corresponding to equal coexistence of two networks, hence $\rho_1 = \rho_2 \neq 0$, is stable as before for values of σ below some critical value σ_c. However, in this regime now the domination solutions ($\rho_1 = 0 \vee \rho_2 = 0$, denoted by the red squares in Fig. 3 (middle, left)) are unstable. This means that, independently from the initial conditions, in this regime the system always approaches the coexistence solution. For $\sigma > \sigma_c$, the equal coexistence solution becomes unstable and new stable solutions emerge (green diamonds in Fig. 3 (middle, right)). These unequal coexistence solutions correspond to the case that one network has a significantly higher activity than the other, but the activities of both networks are sustained. Let us again consider the explicit example of two networks and start with $\sigma > \sigma_c$. The system approaches the equal coexistence solution (green square in Fig. 3 (middle, left)). Then, we change σ to some value above σ_c. Now, the system approaches the unequal coexistence solution (green diamonds in Fig. 3 (middle, right)), but now the activity in both networks is sustained. By lowering σ again below σ_c, the system recovers the equal coexistence solution, in contrast to the previous case. This example is shown in Fig. 3 (bottom) where we present the fraction of active users in both networks. To conclude, in contrast to the case discussed before, the system is robust in the sense that an irreversible loss of digital diversity cannot occur.

---

[8] Here we present only a brief discussion of the dynamical system given by Eqs. (1) and (2). A more detailed analysis and the investigation of different forms of the incentive term in Eq. (2) is left for future research.

[9] Note that here we describe an idealized system without noise. Noise in real systems would speed up significantly the separation of the trajectories in Fig. 2 (bottom) shortly after the first dashed gray line.

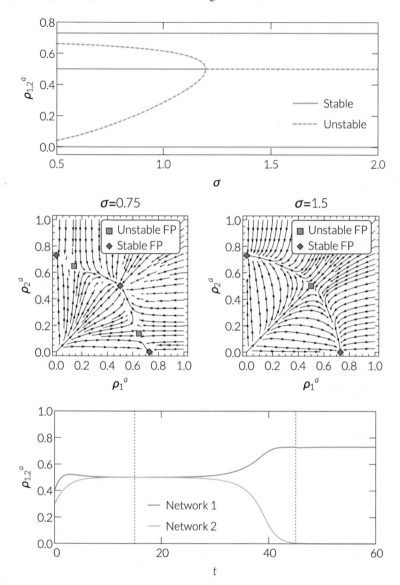

Fig. 2 Fragility of digital diversity. Here, we consider two networks, $\lambda\langle k\rangle = 2$ and $\xi = 0.2$. Top: bifurcation diagram (subcritical pitchfork bifurcation). ρ_i^a denotes the fraction of active users in network i. Green solid lines represent stable solutions and red dashed lines correspond to unstable fixed points. Middle: streamline plots for $\sigma = 0.75$ (left) and $\sigma = 1.5$ (right). Bottom: evolution of the system for initial conditions $\rho_1^a = 0.4$, $\rho_2^a = 0.3$. For $15 \leq t < 45$ (between the dashed lines) we set $\sigma = 1.5$, and otherwise, we set $\sigma = 0.75$

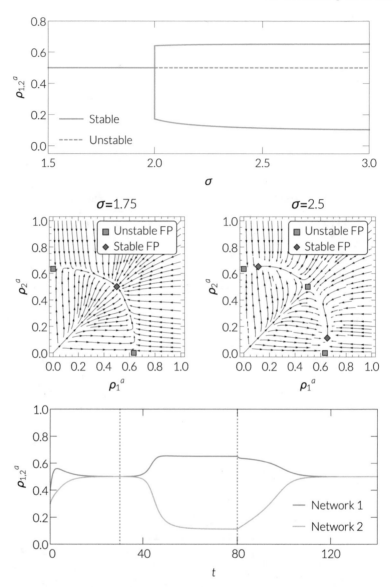

Fig. 3 Robustness of digital diversity. Here, we consider two networks, $\lambda \langle k \rangle = 2$ and $\xi = 1.0$. Top: bifurcation diagram. ρ_i^a denotes the fraction of active users in network i. Green solid lines represent stable solutions and red dashed lines correspond to unstable fixed points. For better readability, here we do not show the unstable fixed points for $\rho_1^a = 0$ and $\rho_2^a = 0$. Middle: streamline plots for $\sigma = 0.75$ (left) and $\sigma = 2.5$ (right). Bottom: evolution of the system for initial conditions $\rho_1^a = 0.4$, $\rho_2^a = 0.3$. For $30 \leq t < 80$ (between the dashed lines), we set $\sigma = 2.5$, and otherwise, we set $\sigma = 1.75$

To sum up, the introduction of a multidimensional incentive system in which one dimension represents socio-digital capital in terms of Social Bitcoins that can be mined by performing search and navigation tasks in a future digital world can make digital diversity robust—given that the value of Social Bitcoins is high enough.

Outlook and Future Research Directions

A multidimensional financial system offers manifold success opportunities for individuals, companies, and states. Top-down control alone is destined to fail in a hyper-connected world. Hence, we need a new approach that incorporates the bottom-up empowerment of society and the right incentives and feedback mechanisms to promote creativity and innovations. The initiative "A nation of makers" [37] in the USA as well as the rise of citizen science [38] constitutes promising starting points for such a development. Nevertheless, increasing financial instabilities emphasize the pressing need to redesign certain aspects of the financial system, hence the urge to create "Finance 4.0" [22].

In this perspective, multiple monetary dimensions could represent different externalities (negative ones like noise, environmental damage, etc., and positive ones such as recycling of resources, cooperation, creation of new jobs, and so on). Building on this framework, appropriate feedback and coordination mechanisms could increase resource efficiency and lead to a more sustainable, circular, cooperative economy. This can be achieved in a bottom-up way in terms of an improved version of capitalism based on the abilities of self-organization intrinsically present in dynamical complex systems by accounting for externalities in a multidimensional incentive system. The Internet of Things and the blockchain technology underlying the Bitcoin architecture provide the technological requirements to realize "Finance 4.0" and "Capitalism 2.0" based on knowledge from the science of complex systems [20–23, 39].

Nowadays, the digital and physical world are strongly interdependent. We have presented an example how a multidimensional incentive system, in particular a Social Bitcoin generated in a bottom-up way by performing search and navigation tasks in a possible future digital world can sustain digital diversity, which is essential for the freedom of information. Furthermore, a diverse digital landscape is expected to create business opportunities for individuals and companies [4, 21, 39] facing the disappearance of half of today's jobs [40]. The price of Social Bitcoins is crucial for the desired effect of sustaining digital diversity. This price, however, is determined dynamically by the market and may depend on other dimensions of the currency system. The development of a concise and general theory of this system and possible implementations comprise interesting future research directions.

References

1. D. Helbing, Nature **497**, 51 (2013)
2. S.V. Buldyrev, R. Parshani, G. Paul, H.E. Stanley, S. Havlin, Nature **464**, 1025 (2010)
3. D. Helbing, *Interaction Support Processor* (2015). https://patentscope.wipo.int/search/en/det
ail.jsf?docId=WO2015118455
4. D. Helbing, Why We Need a New Economy to Survive (2016). https://www.youtube.com/
watch?v=2SeLm5xbnLY
5. D. Helbing, *Social Self-Organization* (Springer, 2012)
6. D. Helbing, The self-organizing society—taking the future in our hands (2015). http://futurict.
blogspot.com/2015/01/the-self-organizing-society-taking.html
7. S.E. Page, *The Difference: How the Power of Diversity Creates Better Groups, Firms, Schools,
and Societies* (Princeton Univ. Press, 2008)
8. J. Arpe, *To the Man with a Hammer: Augmenting the Policymaker's Toolbox for a Complex
World* (Bertelsmann Stiftung, 2016)
9. D. Helbing, Implementing change in a complex world—responding to complexity in socio-
economic systems: How to build a smart and resilient society? (2015). http://futurict.blogspot.
com/2015/03/implementing-change-in-complex-world.html
10. K.K. Kleineberg, M. Boguñá, Sci. Rep. **5**, 10268 (2015)
11. K.-K. Kleineberg, M. Boguñá, Sci. Rep. **6**, 25116 (2016)
12. P. Bak, C. Tang, K. Wiesenfeld, Phys. Rev. Lett. **59**, 381 (1987)
13. Reuters. Negative rates for 2–3 years become worry for banks (Apr 7 2016). http://www.reu
ters.com/article/eurozone-ecb-policy-idUSF9N12D02K
14. Reuters. (Mar 23 2016). http://www.reuters.com/article/us-eurozone-bonds-ecbiduskcn0w
p1o3
15. Reuters. Ecb's credibility at stake if inflation target missed (Apr 7 2016). http://www.reuters.
com/article/eurozone-ecb-inflation-idUSF9N13T000
16. Reuters. ECB could give 1,300 euros to bloc's citizens, Nordea says (Mar 31 2016). http://
www.reuters.com/article/ecb-policy-cash-idUSL5N1733LR
17. M. Lynn, Draghi may have to throw money out of a helicopter (March 2016). http://www.tel
egraph.co.uk/business/2016/03/07/draghi-may-have-to-throw-money-out-of-a-helicopter/
18. Reuters. Fed signals caution on rate hikes, worried by global growth: minutes. http://www.reu
ters.com/article/us-fed-minutes-idUSKCN0X32AB
19. D. Helbing, *Thinking Ahead—Essays on Big Data, Digital Revolution, and Participatory
Market Society* (Springer, 2015)
20. D. Helbing, From communism 2.0 to capitalism 2.0 (March 2016). http://futurict.blogspot.
com/2016/03/from-communism-20-to-capitalism-20.html
21. D. Helbing, Beyond superintelligence: Mastering future challenges with capitalism 2.0 and
democracy 2.0 (2016). https://www.youtube.com/watch?v=OV_b3b_Spow
22. D. Helbing, Qualified money: A better financial system for the future (October 2014). http://
futurict.blogspot.com/2014/10/qualified-money-better-financial-system.html
23. D. Helbing, Why we need democracy 2.0 and capitalism 2.0 to survive (2016). http://futurict.
blogspot.com/2016/04/why-we-need-democracy-20-and-capitalism.html
24. S. Nakamoto, Bitcoin: A peer-to-peer electronic cash system. provides a portrait of what bitcoin
is and how it would be implemented (2009). http://www.bitcoin.org/bitcoin.pdf
25. R. Epstein, R.E. Robertson, Proc. Natl. Acad. Sci. **112**, E4512 (2015)
26. R.M. Bond et al., Nature **489**, 295 (2012)
27. Cyber crime costs projected to reach $2 trillion by 2019 (2016). http://www.forbes.com/sites/
stevemorgan/2016/01/17/cyber-crime-costs-projected-to-reach-2-trillion-by-2019/
28. D. Helbing, E. Pournaras, Nature **527**, 33 (2015)
29. J.L. Contreras, J.H. Reichman, Science **350**, 1312 (2015)
30. isocial, Decentralized online social networks project (2013–2016). http://isocial-itn.eu/
31. https://en.wikipedia.org/wiki/Web_2.0 (2016)

32. S. Aghaei, M.A. Nematbakhsh, H.K. Farsani, Int. J. Web Semant. Technol. **3**, 1 (2012)
33. K.-K. Kleineberg, M. Boguñá, M. ´Angeles Serrano, F. Papadopoulos, Nat. Phys. **12**, 1076 (2016)
34. A. Gulyás, J.J. Bíró, A. Korösi, G. Rétvári, D. Krioukov, Nat. Commun. **6**, 7651 (2015)
35. K.-K. Kleineberg, M. Boguñá, Phys. Rev. X **4**, (2014)
36. B. Ribeiro, Modeling and predicting the growth and death of membership-based websites. Int World Wide Web Conf (2014)
37. A nation of makers (the white house) (2016). https://www.whitehouse.gov/nation-of-makers
38. E. Hand, Nature **466**, 685 (2010)
39. D. Helbing, How the internet of things can make the invisible hand work and societies thrive (2016). http://futurict.blogspot.com.es/2016/02/how-internet-of-things-can-make.html
40. C.B. Frey et al., The future of employment: how susceptible are jobs to computerisation? (2013). http://www.oxfordmartin.ox.ac.uk/downloads/academic/The_Future_of_Employment.pdf

Finance 4.0—A Socio-Ecological Finance System

Mark C. Ballandies, Marcus M. Dapp, Benjamin Aaron Degenhart, Dirk Helbing, Stefan Klauser, and Anabele-Linda Pardi

Abstract *This contribution develops the framework of a novel, socio-ecological finance system that enables the incentivization of environmentally friendly behavior, socially responsible production, resource recycling, sharing and more. We call this system Finance 4.0—where Finance 1.0 refers to a physical coin-based system, Finance 2.0 to a fiat currency system, Finance 3.0 to blockchain finance, while Finance 4.0 stands for a multi-dimensional, real-time feedback system that combines blockchain technology with the Internet of Things. Instead of "Finance 4.0," we will also often use the abbreviation "FIN4."*

In comparison with citizen scores such as the Chinese social credit score, the FIN4 approach is different in a variety of aspects:

- *FIN4 is not aimed at punishment and control, but rather at helping to encourage, empower and coordinate sustainable and other favorable action.*
- *It is being built for local, temporary measurements and feedback, not for global surveillance and control.*
- *It seeks to protect the privacy of people rather than to keep information about everyone and every action forever.*
- *It is not focused on the individual in the sense of profiling and targeting, but on favorable interactions and our social and environmental goals.*
- *It offers a multi-dimensional choice of options instead of trying to determine every individual's action through behavioral manipulation and control.*
- *It has a participatory opt-in nature, where people can co-create the incentive system in such a way that they can reach their goals more successfully.*

A previous version of this chapter has been published as a technical report entitled "FuturICT 2.0: Towards a sustainable digital society with a socio-ecological finance system (Finance 4.0)", accessible here: http://ebook.finfour.net.

M. C. Ballandies · M. M. Dapp (✉) · B. A. Degenhart · D. Helbing · S. Klauser · A.-L. Pardi
Computational Social Science, Stampfenbachstrasse 48, 8092 Zurich, Switzerland
e-mail: mdapp@ethz.ch

M. M. Dapp et al. (eds.), *Finance 4.0—Towards a Socio-Ecological Finance System*,
SpringerBriefs in Applied Sciences and Technology,
https://doi.org/10.1007/978-3-030-71400-0_4

- *With multi-dimensional incentivization, it becomes possible to advance several goals simultaneously; thereby, many more people can benefit from the interactions they engage in, as multi-dimensional value exchange increases the solution space enormously.*

Keywords Blockchain · Sustainability · Decentralized governance · Incentive system · Value-sensitive design · Cryptoeconomics

The Finance 4.0 Ambition

The world is facing existential threats. These challenges are putting pressure on our economy, society and environment. The unresolved problems of the 2008 financial crisis still endanger the economic stability of Europe and the world. Currently, many nation states struggle to control the power of major banks and global corporations. We are told to accept they are "too big to fail"—thereby skewing incentives and creating moral hazards.

Digitization and globalization are increasingly creating an interconnected world. While this process has brought much progress and improved the standard of living, it has also produced new threats, in particular a crisis in terms of sustainability.

The globalized economy now comprises a massive, complex network of systems that is much harder to map and control than the economies of the twentieth century. One of the critical problems is that today's economic order is creating systemic market failures due to all sorts of unwanted externalities. A concerted global effort to regulate and account for these externalities is yet to be seen. Pricing externalities in dollars, for example, is not expected to be sufficient. As a result, a series of ecological and economic crises threaten the very basis upon which our economy and society are built (Fig. 1).

What is more, access to scarce resources is becoming a growing concern. The use of fossil fuels and raw materials has tripled in the last 40 years [1], and climate change may lead to the extinction of one sixth of all species [2]. Not to mention the additional challenges posed by war, terrorism and the migration of displaced people. At every scale, individual incentives today are often misaligned with the core values of our societies. As a consequence, the world suffers from an overall lack of sustainability. How should we tackle this web of interdependent, complex crises and mitigate some of the fundamental challenges humanity faces? This is where FuturICT 2.0 comes in. The project pursued disruptive innovation to address the root cause of these problems—a lack of sustainability—by combining the Internet of Things, blockchain technology and complexity science to open up new opportunities.

In alignment with the UN Sustainable Development Goals (and future iterations thereof), our proposal called "Finance 4.0" concerns a multi-dimensional incentive system to manage complex systems and promote a circular and sharing economy. The aim is to create a high quality of life for more people with fewer resources by aligning

Fig. 1 Ecological footprints of selected countries (National Footprint Assessments 2017, Global Footprint Network)

individual incentives with core values—defined and driven by the communities themselves.

Finance 4.0 (short FIN4) encompasses a socio-ecological finance system, a novel economic system and a new social contract. With respect to finance, we propose a multi-dimensional cryptocurrency ecosystem promoting decentralization and positive action. Regarding the economy, we suggest a new, privacy-preserving incentivization scheme influencing production and consumption in a way that will promote a circular and sharing economy. This new system should be held together by a new kind of social contract fostering community-based decision-making, allowing for subsidiarity as well as local and personal diversity.

FIN4 is democratic, pluralistic and inclusive. It leverages information and communication systems to empower everyone to take better decisions, be more creative, and coordinate or cooperate with others—thereby leading to better business models, products and services, smarter cities and smarter societies.

FIN4 is ambitious. Globally, we face what we could describe as a misalignment of goals and incentive structures. There are some common goals with respect to sustainability: the United Nations Sustainable Development Goals (SDGs) [3] and the Paris Agreement [4]. However, while agreeing on a joint set of supranational goals is certainly important, it marks only the first step in a long and challenging transition.

How to translate global goals into individual incentives and collective actions? The first pillar builds on the concept of nation states, which internalize the global targets by integrating them into their national legislation. This regulation-based approach is undoubtedly the most commonly considered when discussing the need for more sustainability, but it seems to be too slow.

The second pillar builds on mostly voluntary, often profit-driven contributions or on self-restraint of global corporations. However, this proves inefficient so far. By now, it is clear that these pillars alone are insufficient to make our world more sustainable quickly enough.[1]

We therefore propose a third pillar, based on "co-opetition": individual contributions that are coordinated and assisted digitally, which is the basis of the FIN4 system and the Climate City Cup.[2]

In order to develop this concept, accompanied by basic research in the respective fields, FuturICT 2.0 has proposed to develop a FIN4 demonstrator. This demonstrator should show that, with modern technology, it is feasible to create an environment that fosters sustainability without compromising human rights and subsidiarity. Its goal is to illustrate the possibility of an innovative framework with features such as the following:

- the ability to create bottom-up money similar to Bitcoin,
- multi-dimensional money exchange with multiple currencies representing various environmental, social and other kinds of values and costs,
- the use of this system to price and trade externalities of different kinds,
- suitable incentive mechanisms enabling a favorable (self-)organization of socio-economic systems on different scales,
- feedbacks promoting a circular and sharing economy,
- the possibility of taxation.

To achieve these goals, we wanted to combine the following technologies and principles:

- decentralized currencies and blockchain technology to enable reliable peer-to-peer contracts, allowing the creation of a direct and sustainable sharing economy,
- sensors and the Internet of Things (IoT) to make it possible to measure externalities and build a circular economy, with various externalities represented by different currencies complementing the current monetary system,
- specific community-based incentives to support the self-organization of complex systems and help them evolve towards a circular economy; more efficient use of resources by promoting social cooperation and climate protection,
- research could be conducted in many areas. Among other fields, the team has explored Distributed Ledger Technology (DLT) systems, behavioral economics, cryptoeconomic design, requirements design, proof mechanisms, identity and governance (see the Glossary for an explanation of special terms).

---

[1] cf. https://climateactiontracker.org/countries/.

[2] cf. https://climatecitycup.org.

The Finance 4.0 Framework

One of the reasons for unsustainable behavior is the long period of time between our actions and the consequences they may have. For instance, people have been burning coal for two centuries and driving motor vehicles for one century, while carbon dioxide emissions have only recently been considered to be a serious global problem. Such circumstances create cognitive dissonance, i.e., an uncomfortable feeling of inconsistency.

FIN4 aims to create a self-organizing, highly nuanced incentive system that supports the daily decision-making of people by encouraging desirable actions and discouraging undesirable behaviors.

To promote sustainability, it is important that the FIN4 system takes externalities into account. However, the FIN4 system does this by *multiple* currencies, reflecting different societal values. By giving externalities prices and allowing them to be traded, they can be internalized to reflect costs and benefits more accurately in a multi-dimensional way. Externalities can be positive (like certain kinds of innovation or infrastructure) or negative (such as pollution).

FIN4 focuses primarily on positive action, rather than on sanctions, for the following reasons:

As an opt-in system, it would be almost impossible to motivate participants to join if they would face a negative balance of tokens, taking into account negative externalities. Obtaining tokens for positive action is a much better value proposition. FIN4, therefore, focuses on rewards for positive actions, rather than on punishments for negative actions.

Our daily choices often seem to be detached from our values. Using a smart distributed incentive system, however, communities can reward what they value—by issuing new types of tokens to address local needs.

These positive actions can be whatever the community considers to be valuable. Examples may include planting trees, using a bike rather than a car, helping a person in need or recycling.

In this case, the tokens can take on any form of value for the communities. They can be fully symbolic (imagine a virtual trophy representing a tree you have planted), give access to a service (such as free bicycle maintenance) or even have a monetary value.

The core process of FIN4 is illustrated in Fig. 2.

A new type of token is created with a name, a short ticker symbol (similar to "USD" or "BTC") and a statement describing the purpose of the token. Users can record actions and then claim the respective tokens. A claim may be verified in three different ways, which can be combined with each other:

- *sensor proofs* use data transmitted from an IoT sensor or device for location, humidity or temperature, for example. This includes mobile proofs from a user's smartphone (such as photographic documentation).
- *social proofs* mean other users attest that a certain action has been performed.

Fig. 2 Rewarding positive actions is the core of Finance 4.0

- *third-party data proofs* utilize external sources of data, where this cannot be generated within the FIN4 system directly (Fig. 3).

Let us here discuss the example of litter disposal.

Alice creates a type of token for incentivizing people to pick up and dispose of litter they find in public parks. The community collectively likes this idea and adopts it. While hiking, Bob finds an empty plastic bottle and takes a couple of photos showing where he found it and where he disposed of it. Bob uploads these pictures to the claiming platform and other users approve his claim, rewarding him with a number of positive action tokens.

Sensor or mobile proofs require security measures in the hardware or software to prevent cheating, such as double claiming. Social proofs need an additional incentive

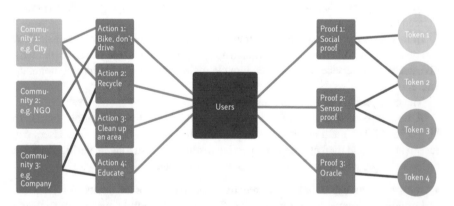

Fig. 3 Communities create tokens to represent positive actions. Users prove to the system that they performed such actions to receive the respective tokens

layer that motivates other users to provide attestations in good faith, while also preventing collusion.

Placing real-life data on the blockchain is a non-trivial problem and can be susceptible to manipulation or mistakes. In practice, it will likely require combinations of these proofs (like in our example above) in order to adequately prevent cheating. After all, data may not necessarily represent the truth of real-world actions. An oracle based on third-party data might be required to prove that submitted data is correct, before it is irrevocably placed on an immutable blockchain. Once a claim has been proven using these approaches—or indeed combinations of them—the tokens are minted and transferred to the claiming user.

The prover may be the token's creator, a dedicated group of people (such as token holders) or any random user, depending on the nature of the action and type of token. The most effective and useful token systems will likely be approved and adopted by the community in a self-organized and self-sustaining manner.

We envision a multi-layered, multi-dimensional system of decentralized digital cryptocurrencies created at different levels with different characteristics, serving different purposes.

The token systems may operate at a supranational, regional or local level. The different purposes may address environmental, social or other values relevant for sustainability or society.

The FIN4 core system comprises a token economy and a governance framework. The token economy gradually emerges as communities asynchronously create, obtain and trade positive action tokens, thereby creating a market for these positive actions.

In order to align user incentives towards the creation of this market, a governance layer is needed that supports the development of a healthy token economy. This governance layer uses a governance token (GOV) to offer mechanisms that allow users to collectively decide on which tokens to promote as "official FIN4 tokens" (Fig. 4).

Any system that allows users to propose new token designs will have to deal with the problem of spam. So, how can we ensure our ecosystem promotes useful token concepts? Rather than establishing rules and barriers to restrict the creation of tokens, our design leverages the innovative capacity of independent token proposals. Every token idea is welcome, but acceptance as an official FIN4 token requires users to vote for it with their governance (GOV) tokens. Thus, all users co-maintain a list of approved positive action tokens.

The *reputation* tokens (REP) to facilitate social proofs do not yet exist in our system. Their purpose is to help users establish trust in one another in order to interact effectively on the platform. Reputation should reflect the support of the system by the user (e.g., proving, voting, etc.) and not their actual positive action token holdings, which could otherwise introduce bias to the reputation system.

In our current design, users obtain reputation tokens by performing actions that support and strengthen the entire FIN4 system. As a minimum, the actions suitable for obtaining these reputation tokens include (1) the active gathering of tokens (low

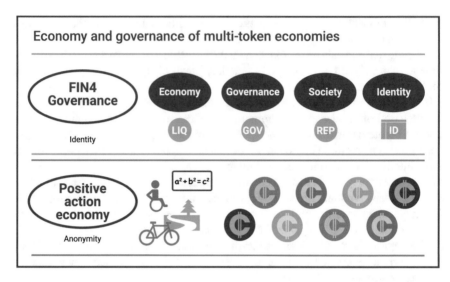

Fig. 4 Human coordination in FIN4's multi-token economy happens on two levels

reward), (2) participation in proof mechanisms (medium reward) and (3) the acceptance of token designs by curators (high reward). Finally, users should also be able
to lose these reputation tokens.

Also, how can we incentivize entire communities that may already have their own
tokens established to join the larger ecosystem? The idea is to represent the additional
liquidity won when joining the larger FIN4 network through a "reserve currency"
we call liquidity token (LIQ). This token would stand for the network effects gained
when enabling larger networks and markets.

One conceivable, yet too simplistic approach would be to create the same number
of FIN4 tokens for each accepted token proposal. The overall number of liquidity
tokens would, therefore, be commensurate with the total number of FIN4 tokens in
the system, thereby giving users more trust in using the different tokens and some
assurance that tokens can be exchanged with one another. This could be based on the
original idea of "Bancor" by John Maynard Keynes; however, the final design has
not yet been decided.

Due to the nature of blockchain technology, blockchain creators are unable to
prevent trades beyond the confines of the system. Our approach is to create strong
incentives to use the platform, while preserving the freedom of users to leave at any
time and take their token balances with them.

Furthermore, a form of *identity* is needed when users wish to participate in the
governance of FIN4. Identity (ID) here corresponds less to the idea of a scanned
passport and more to a concept of self-sovereignty built entirely within the FIN4
system or transferred from other platforms. For example, reputation mechanims may
establish identity over time.

Distributed Ledger Technology (DLT)

What definitions are currently used in practice for concepts like tokens, transactions and consensus? And what exactly is distributed ledger technology (DLT)?

The blockchain community still suffers from a general lack of a shared understanding of terminology, making comparisons between different blockchain-based projects difficult. To support a common understanding (and as part of our research towards the FIN4 system), we developed a systematic taxonomy of distributed ledger systems [5].

Accordingly, we define distributed ledger technology (DLT) as a range of distributed data structures in which entries are recorded by participants after reaching consensus on their validity. A consensus mechanism—the set of rules for transaction validation—is integrated into a DLT system to ensure system reliability, where no trusted third parties are required to authorize or validate entries. Distributed ledgers often support secure token economies. These rely on digital tokens and cryptographic techniques to determine how to perform exchange between participants. The most well-known and successful example of a DLT system is Bitcoin.

While the taxonomy paper mentioned above provides a more extensive introduction to the topic, a conceptual architecture of distributed ledger technology is shown in the figure below.

Incentivization may occur on either the consensus or action layer. The first generation of blockchains are known as cryptocurrencies. They are chiefly based on incentive systems that maintain consensus mechanisms in the digital world.

The second generation of blockchain projects are based on smart contract engines allowing for the creation of tokens. These tokens can be utilized to incentivize people or machines to perform certain actions in the real world. One example for a token standard that creates fungible (exchangeable) tokens is the widely used ERC20 token standard on the Ethereum smart contract platform[3]—also used as a basis for our positive action tokens in the FIN4 system.

FIN4 takes full advantage of this possibility by not only creating a range of platform tokens used for governance, but also by offering users mechanisms to create tokens as they wish (Fig. 5).

The taxonomy paper categorizes different examples of existing tokens by means of several attributes [5]. These attributes include the underlying source of value of the token, the regulation of action/read permissions, the supply policy, the transferability and the condition governing the minting of new tokens. It also covers the various consensus mechanisms that exist, such as "proof of work" or "proof of stake."

The FIN4 system will foster communities that can create and use tokens to promote the sustainable action they consider important, following a consensus framework we like to call *"proof of good work."*

Many aspects of cryptoeconomic design will be available to these communities when creating token proposals. Community members will be able to configure a

---

[3] cf. www.ethereum.org.

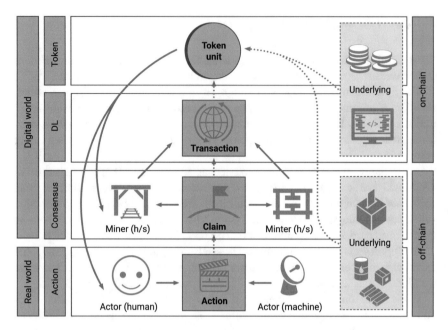

Fig. 5 Conceptual architecture of distributed ledger systems, based on [5]

range of token attributes. For example, what is the claiming process? Who is able to approve claims? And how many tokens should be minted for every verified positive action?

Value-Sensitive Design

The world faces major challenges as a consequence of insufficient sustainability. We assume that current economic incentives, which fail to effectively reward sustainable behavior, are partly responsible for this problem.

Sustainability

One of the key objectives of the FIN4 platform is to address sustainability issues and reduce negative environmental externalities with positive action. We hope to achieve this by creating a system that enables communities to define sustainable and socially desirable actions and to reward individuals who align their behavior with these goals, using exchangeable incentive tokens. Note, however, that not everyone needs to engage in the same kinds of actions to be rewarded. On the contrary: the system supports specific actions fitting personal preferences and talents. In this regard, the multi-dimensionality of the approach is highly relevant.

Inclusion

In order to achieve this transformation towards a world, which is more aware of sustainability, the FIN4 system follows a bottom-up approach that enables everyone to participate, contribute their own ideas and protect the system for the benefit of the community.

Communities should not only be able to determine the values and token concepts most important to them, but also to shape how the platform develops. The users themselves will also be essential for maintaining the system and for protecting it from abuse via the reputation tokens. These tokens will enable every user to have a say on which token proposals to accept. However, the weight that their votes carry will depend on how trustworthy their conduct has been so far.

Freedom

We believe that people should be encouraged, not compelled, to participate, which speaks for an opt-in platform. Users would be able to interact with the FIN4 platform as long as they wish—and also leave, whenever they want, perhaps even with the possibility to take their token holdings with them.

The decentral nature of permissionless DLT—for both data storage and decision-making—is intended to prevent a single point of failure or authority. This provides protection against censorship, inappropriate control, or other arbitrary interventions, since data is stored immutably on the blockchain.

User identities are pseudonymous, thereby protecting the privacy of individuals. Anonymity is an essential requirement of democratic systems with privacy protection. It allows participants to engage in independent decision-making.

The pursuit of multiple objectives can, however, result in conflicting goals, which we have realized in a dedicated ethics workshop with ethix.[4] We attempt to minimize such conflicts using appropriate coordination mechanisms and, where they are too limited, suitable governance. We outline these ethical considerations below.

Preventing Misuse

We do not dictate what behavior we consider socially desirable. Instead, we leave this decision to the community. So, how to prevent misuse of the platform? If users acted in bad faith or for their own purely selfish interests, they may indeed start to reward actions with tokens that do not accord with the moral principles of the project. Such misuse would not only harm the FIN4 community, it might also have wider consequences for society.

---

[4]cf. www.ethix.ch.

Nonetheless, we trust that a critical mass of users can prevent such misuse, as they have the power to vote down token proposals created in bad faith. Trustworthy users—i.e., those with more reputation tokens—will have a greater voice in determining the list of official tokens. This mechanism can also avoid excessive spam in the system.

Ensuring Democratic Legitimacy

The inclusive and voluntary nature of the platform means that the issuance of tokens will be legitimized by a high level of participation, with decision-making being subject to voting.

However, there is a risk that a consistent majority will end up holding a position of power, such that individuals with minority positions may be discriminated against to some degree. This could be exacerbated—to some extent—by reputation tokens, as they would allow trusted groups to accumulate voting power.

In order to prevent a scenario in which a majority suppresses minorities from happening, a maximum number of reputation tokens should be defined—with no user being able to hold more than this limit. This would help to contain the risk that a certain group accumulates too much power (see also the subsection below on "Governance").

Avoiding Social Pressure

While we hope that FIN4 proves useful in promoting a sustainable society and that the platform enjoys widespread adoption, we realize that mass adoption could result in growing social pressure on non-users to join the platform. This would question the voluntary nature of the platform.

Those who choose not to participate may face exclusion from certain kinds of transactions—a situation that might put the core value of freedom at risk and would have to be counteracted.

Governance

There are also important ethical considerations in terms of platform governance.

Once the platform is launched, the integrated governance mechanisms will largely determine the success of FIN4—especially as we will then cede the content and structure to the community, losing our ability to make subsequent changes.

Anticipating these potential risks ahead of time is key. Therefore, our approach to governance includes the following:

- **Blockchain:** This technology permits decentralized decision-making as well as transparent data storage. The security risk is distributed across the network and, thereby, minimized. Furthermore, pseudonymous participation as implied by a public blockchain is compatible with the core values of inclusion, privacy and freedom.

- **Openness:** The platform is open to anyone who wishes to participate. This is intended to legitimize the new decision-making processes.
- **Community moderation:** A hierarchy will emerge between users with different balances of reputation tokens, which are given to those users who commit time and effort to the platform. These tokens will help protect the platform from malicious actors. The combination of inclusion and a time- and effort-based hierarchy may produce both meritocratic and democratic effects. What is more, the use of procedures like "quadratic voting" would reduce the risk of certain users accumulating too much voting power.

The Cryptoeconomic Design of Finance 4.0

Relevance of Cryptoeconomic Design

As mentioned earlier in the DLT taxonomy section, there is a lack of commonly agreed terms in this field. This is also true for the term "cryptoeconomics." Vitalik Buterin—the founder of Ethereum—posited that cryptoeconomics is a discipline that combines cryptographic proofs of past events with economic incentives to encourage future events as part of a blockchain system [6].

The cryptographic components mainly encompass consensus algorithms, enabled by digital signatures and hash functions, and have more recently progressed to include zero-knowledge proofs, multi-party computation and homomorphic encryption [7]. The economic components involve principles of game theory, mechanism design and network economics. As explaining all these terms is out of scope of this book, we recommend interested readers to consult the references to get a better understanding of them. In a nutshell, the aim of applied cryptoeconomics is to design new economies based on cryptographic tokens and mechanisms in order to create incentive systems for users.

Web 2.0 applications (known as Apps) refer to platforms like Facebook, Google or Amazon. These are to be contrasted with the emerging Web 3.0—and Decentralized Applications (known as DApps)—which are relevant to FIN4. Decentralized Applications run on peer-to-peer networks, where no node typically enjoys privileges over other nodes. This is quite unlike Web 2.0 Apps controlled by a central provider. While both cases require functional and error-free code, this is not enough for the Web 3.0. That is because DApps encode economic incentives using smart contracts in order to incentivize certain actions. In the example of Bitcoin, miners are rewarded with newly mined Bitcoins for successfully mining a new block. These mechanisms are cryptographically protected and practically impossible to change. As a consequence, modifications to the software require the coordinated effort of all nodes. If only a majority of nodes cooperate, rather than all, the network runs the risk of diverging in a "fork."

Even if the code of DApps is flawless, the decentralized system may still fail due to the mechanisms built into the network, if they are based on inaccurate assumptions about individual or collective user behavior. This is particularly true if the system neglects to consider potential misuse, malicious action, or user mistakes. Effective crypoteconomic design (CED), therefore, needs to take all this into account (Fig. 6).

Effective CED is important for several reasons. First of all, implementing the values of a developer community into individual incentives for a larger user base is rather difficult. Good cryptoeconomic design seeks to reduce the potential for incentive misalignment at the various levels of the system as illustrated in the following figure based on Zargham [8]. The framework is useful for analyzing CED systems by highlighting the interconnections: five distinct layers, with each layer requiring the layer beneath and enabling the layer above.

Second, effective CED is vital since the possibilities to implement subsequent changes or corrections to a live DApp are very limited. Smart contracts written on a blockchain can neither be stopped nor modified easily.

Third, CED needs to take into account the challenge of designing a complex system. Here, multiple variables and interrelationships come into play, which allow for suitable self-organization and emergence of behavioral patterns.

Fig. 6 Creating interconnected collaborative communities (based on [8])

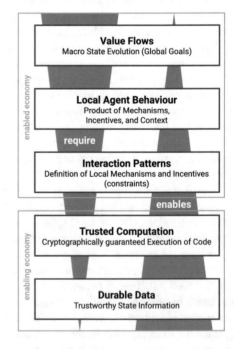

Fourth, cryptoeconomic design must reflect the implicit objective of cryptoeconomic systems to translate the values of a community into specific incentives for individuals. For instance, the Bitcoin community values secure and non-censorable transactions above everything else. The system, therefore, promotes decentralized mining to run the transactions. On the other hand, minimizing energy consumption was not considered an important value in the Bitcoin community and no incentive—other than waste minimization/profit maximization for miners—was therefore established to pursue it. The heated debate whether Bitcoin wastes energy or pushes the price of renewables close to zero over time, resulting in a net positive effect, is still ongoing.

Designing Cryptoeconomic Systems

The problems addressed by cryptoeconomic systems are invariably complex, and, as it is a new field, standard processes for cryptoeconomic design have not yet been established. However, a multi-scale perspective can be adopted to comprehend complex economic and cryptoeconomic systems. Policymakers can seek to change the global system behavior either via enforced rules (which we find problematic) or incentives (which we find more agreeable). These policies affect the local behavior of agents and, in turn, influence global behavior. Nevertheless, designing a cryptoeconomic system that works as intended is a complex problem requiring the configuration of various system attributes such as the permissions in a system, the supply of a token and the type of distributed ledger utilized.

In order to simplify this configuration process, the following three-step methodology can be utilized:

First, the system designer has to map the goals of a cryptoeconomic system to specific requirements of that system. Second, based on these requirements, the designer can utilize Fig. 11 from Dobler et al. [9] to identify the right system layout. Third, once a layout is chosen, the DLT taxonomy mentioned earlier [5] can be used to configure the system layout with the appropriate attributes (Fig. 7).

The Finance 4.0 Token Economy

The FIN4 system is designed to store a variety of information. This includes which tokens have been created, who has claimed which tokens, who has submitted proofs for actions, and who owns which tokens. This balance and tracking information is required for positive action tokens as well as meta tokens for FIN4 governance.

As an open, community-based system, FIN4 allows multiple roles for writing information to the blockchain. Depending on the proof mechanism, for example, any user can approve action proofs by other users. Moreover, users are able to create and

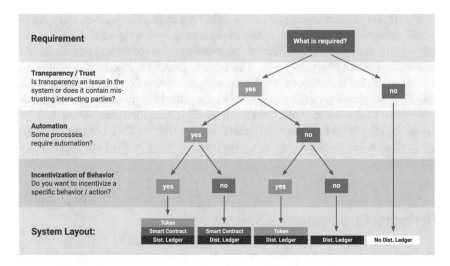

Fig. 7 Impact of system requirements on system layout (based on [5])

obtain positive action tokens anonymously; this helps to make the platform openly accessible.

We have also decentralized the necessary mechanisms to the greatest extent possible, to avoid the need for an "always-online trusted third party."

According to the decision tree proposed by Wüst and Gervais [10], a permission-less blockchain is recommended for such a setup (Fig. 8). FIN4 is built using smart contracts secured by the Ethereum network (a permissionless blockchain system).

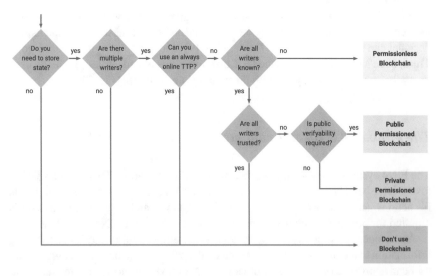

Fig. 8 Decision process for permission types in a Blockchain-based system (based on [10])

Thus, mapping our system goals and values (see the section on "Value-Sensitive Design") according to the design requirements proposed by Dobler et al. [9], the FIN4 system requirements can be summarized as follows:

- **Transparency:** FIN4 aims to increase the visibility of certain undervalued actions. Many positive things that people do every day go unnoticed as the current monetary system does not ascribe value to this behavior. Visibility is also required in order for markets to emerge for the various positive action tokens, with much of this data stored and tracked on the blockchain.
- **Automation:** FIN4 aims to ensure that all users are treated as equal peers in the system, the rules for creating and obtaining tokens as well as governance need to be codified in a neutral way, with smart contracts.
- **Incentivization:** FIN4 aims to create a multi-dimensional incentive system to encourage more sustainable behavior, rewarding good actions with incentives in the form of various cryptoeconomic tokens.

With these requirements, the FIN4 system layout has to consist of a distributed ledger, smart contracts and cryptoeconomic tokens.

Applying Zargham's layered model (see Fig. 9 and cf. Fig. 6), FIN4 is based on an enabling economy, consisting of a distributed ledger (DL[T]) and smart contracts (SC), ensuring durable data and trusted computation, in a permissionless environment. Above this layer, a set of constraints in the form of local mechanisms

Fig. 9 Interconnected layers of Finance 4.0 as a cryptoeconomic system with tokens representing [official] positive action ([O]PAT), reputation (REP), or governance (GOV)

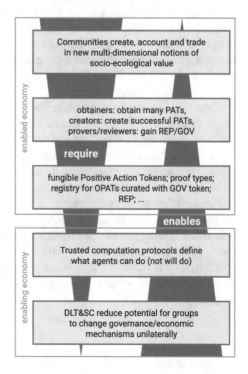

(for actions, proofs and token curation) as well as incentives (to create and obtain tokens and the associated actions) are defined. The different tokens—[official] Positive Action Tokens ([O]PAT), Reputation Tokens (REP), and Governance Tokens (GOV)—allow for complex interaction patterns. Exposing such interactions to the real-world, as defined by the community's needs, should lead to local agent behavior that is conducive to the global goals for the FIN4 system.

FIN4 ultimately aims to enable a new type of economy that better values sustainable action—from the perspective of communities themselves to society at large. This value should not be created in isolation, but result in a flow of values within the network to balance the demand and supply of positive actions, leading to the optimal allocation of resources to achieve global goals of sustainable behavior at scale.

Simulating the Token Design Space

Agent-based modeling (ABM) has been used extensively in the past few years [11–13] as a powerful tool, also in the context of econophysics [14], and especially for market modeling [15, 16]. Moreover, ABM-based computer simulations proved to be useful in the study of socio-economic systems and more [17–19].

Generally, the agents in ABM simulations are given attributes to define their behavior. They can adapt according to situations and interact with each other [20]. In our agent-based approach, we have human agents which fulfill certain roles (like token claimers or token creators) and token-type agents. The FIN4 simulation code is open source and is based on time steps, using cadCAD,[5] an open-source tool for "complex adaptive dynamics computer-aided design". At every time step, key variables are updated through actions or policies.

In addition to being sustainable and scalable, the FIN4 system should also be resilient to unintended user behavior. We use simulations to improve the cryptoeconomic design towards system stability and to avoid dynamics that may result from not fully accounting for the "human factor."

Our definition of an ideal stable system includes token creators with noble intent, tokens invulnerable to manipulation and users using tokens as intended. In contrast, bad situations can occur due to token creators with malicious intent, tokens vulnerable to manipulation, or users cheating.

The simulation configuration allows one to study groups of human users as agents with certain predefined attributes (e.g., intentions, compliance with rules or commitments defining a type of token) or with random attributes. To bootstrap a token-based economy in a community, agents can define types of tokens that will be available for claiming or allowing fellow agents to create their own tokens with a certain frequency.

---

[5]cf. www.cadCAD.org.

Stage	FIN4 Principles	Behavior Expectations	Potential Risks	Mitigation Strategies
0	Anyone can **access**	Many join, users join in bursts (entire communities)	Users flood system with "fake accounts" (sybil attack on access)	Decentralized blockchain: each user needs wallet and crypto for using FIN4
1	Anyone can **obtain** Positive Action Tokens (PATs)	Many different PATs are obtained, a multi-dimensional incentive system unfolds and develops	Users cheat to enrich themselves with PATs	Proof mechanisms: users need to prove to the system that they did actions
2	Anyone can **create** Positive Action Tokens	Dynamic, obtaining tokens happens more often than creating tokens	Spam of PATs in general, spam of malicious PATs	Token Registry: users co-curate list of trustworthy PATs (GOV token needed)
3	Anyone can **curate** Positive Action Tokens	Committed users successively gain influence to co-govern FIN4 system by accumulating GOV tokens.	Users hoard GOV tokens to self-promote own PATs, attack other PATs in teams, or try to amass power.	Individual Reputation: no matter their PAT wealth, users need to build reputation over time to receive GOV tokens. Bad behavior results in reputation loss. (REP token needed)

Fig. 10 Elements of an iterative simulation concept for the Finance 4.0 system with tokens representing positive action (PAT), reputation (REP), or governance (GOV)

Figure 10 illustrates the iterative approach that the simulation concept is built on. The simulation follows the natural stages that users encounter when joining the Fin4 system and accounts for the risks that occur at each stage.

The basic principle of FIN4 is that anyone can access the system (stage 0). Depending on their intentions, users may enter individually or as a "cartel" in a coordinated fashion to unduly influence the system. The main safeguard against this is to use blockchain technology: Wallets and keys represent barriers and prevent users from spamming (e.g., auto-registering many fake users).

Once they entered the system (stage 1), users can obtain Positive Action Tokens (PATs) at their own discretion. The core problem here is cheating: Users try to obtain tokens without performing the required actions. Therefore, an extendable set of proof mechanisms is put in place to support the process of proving actions. As anyone is able to create new types of Positive Action Tokens (PATs, stage 2), the system may face a flood of PATs. To navigate the token space and avoid malicious tokens to gain traction, users co-curate tokens and promote the trustworthy ones. As anyone is able to participate in token curation (stage 3), more complex types of malicious behavior are thinkable. To counter them, a reputation mechanism is put in place to steer how users gain power for co-governance over time.

For the evaluation of the system's state, we identified a series of behavioral and design parameters and visualized them as dimensions of a three-dimensional parameter space (see Fig. 11).

Obtainer compliance: "1" means that token obtainers respect and fulfill the token proof type according to the demands of the token creator. "−1" means that all the

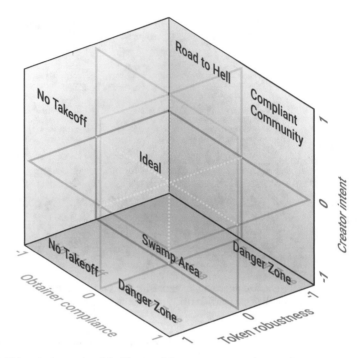

Fig. 11 Token design space of the Finance 4.0 system

users find a way to claim the token without doing the action for it, by finding the weak spot of the token proof mechanism and exploiting it.

Token robustness: "1" means that the design of the token proof is so good that it has no weak spots that can be exploited, yet it is simple enough not to hinder users in claiming. "−1" means that the token proof mechanism is flawed and individuals can claim tokens without performing the action the token was created for.

Creator intent: "1" means that the token creator has noble intent when creating the token, e.g., for slowing down climate change, feeding the poor, saving endangered species, etc. "−1" means that the token creator is malicious (usually focused on personal gain), intending, for example, the exploitation of users, the manipulation of public opinion or the destruction of private property.

The "Ideal" region of the parameter space represents the best case in which the users are compliant, the token types have robust proof mechanisms and the intention of the token creator is noble. The "Compliant Community" area is equivalent to the "Ideal" case only when all users are compliant. The "Danger Zones" correspond to worst-case scenarios. They are characterized by the malicious intent of the token creator that can be hidden from the token claimers. On the other hand, the "Road to Hell" area contains tokens created with good intentions that are abused or misused by the community. The "No Takeoff" regions and the "Swamp Area" lack compliance of the users.

At this stage of the simulations, the token types created are mapped to the parameter space according to their attributes (robust or weak design) and the community profile (compliance and intention). So far, the picture is a static one. The next steps are to introduce reputation (and governance) tokens and the Token Curated Registry (TCR). Once human agents will vote for token types according to their interests (using GOV tokens) and will challenge official tokens for the sake of the community (using the TCR), the static picture will become dynamic and PAT types will move from one area in the parameter space to another. Our goal is to study these dynamics and to figure out how we can keep tokens out of the "Danger Zones" and create traction towards the top right corner ("Ideal") (Fig. 11).

In our point of view, the governance of a decentralized system should be based on trust and experience. In order to select the people who will obtain the power to vote on official tokens, we propose constructing a trust network in the community using reputation tokens (REP). Once the network is vast enough (measured in terms of nodes and links between nodes), we focus on key nodes in the newly formed network: the nodes most connected directly to other nodes (Total Degree Centrality), the interfaces between groups (Betweenness Centrality) and the most influential/powerful actors according to the network (Eigenvector Centrality).

The Finance 4.0 Technology Landscape

The Finance 4.0 Architecture

In order to contribute to solving real-world sustainability issues, our ambition was also to lay the groundwork of a system that can survive and thrive under real-world conditions, applying system engineering methods.

As a first step towards developing a demonstrator platform, a series of workshops was conducted, aiming at compiling an initial list of requirements.

Two expert workshops were organized in 2018 to examine a range of specific challenges. A proving workshop in Zurich covered topics relating to the design and use of oracles, while a cryptoeconomics workshop in Berlin discussed some of the decisions made for the incentive system.

Based on the results of the requirements phase and the workshops, a functional architecture was developed to describe the core functionality of FIN4 (see Fig. 12).

The system architecture consists of three main layers (bottom to top):

- **A blockchain layer:** The blockchain including the smart contract engine serves as backbone to make FIN4 a decentralized, peer-to-peer platform. Transactions, data on smart contracts and balances on tokens are stored immutable and tamper-proof on the blockchain ledger.
- **A smart contract layer:** FIN4 smart contracts get deployed onto the blockchain. They comprise both the operation logic and the storage of most of the data. All of the functionality lies here and is accessible even from outside the FIN4 application.

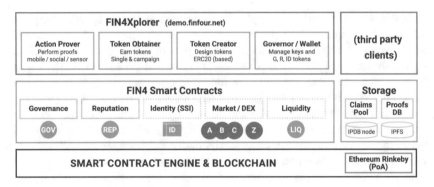

Fig. 12 Functional architecture of the Finance 4.0 system

While most data is stored directly on the contracts, media files provided to proof claims (e.g., a picture of a planted tree) are uploaded to the Inter-Planetary File System (IPFS), and only their identifiers are stored on the smart contract. The claims pool is not yet implemented.

- **An application layer:** The purpose of the application layer is to interface with end users—typically via Web or mobile applications. While a default client for both Web and mobile is provided, third parties can also interface with the system by building their own clients. Thus, they can limit the functionality that the FIN4 smart contracts provide. Extensions to the FIN4 core system, however, can only be made on the smart contract layer.

Suitable programming languages and frameworks have to be defined to implement this functional architecture. For the smart contract engine and blockchain layer, we chose the Ethereum platform.[6] Ethereum is a relatively widespread and established smart contract engine, with a large community of developers and projects, as well as a broad range of development tools.

The FIN4Xplorer is running on the Rinkeby test net.[7] There are currently no plans to make the demonstrator available on Ethereum's main net, as high costs would incur and there would be no immediate gains in functionality or performance. However, projects that follow on from FuturICT 2.0 in the future may choose to take this route.

The FIN4 smart contracts are written in the Solidity programming language[8] and deployed using Truffle[9] as a framework and Infura[10] as a provider.

The FIN4 client we provide is a Web application written in JavaScript[11] using the React library.[12] The layout is optimized for viewing on both desktop and mobile

---

[6]cf. https://ethereum.org/.

[7]cf. https://rinkeby.io.

[8]cf. https://soliditylang.org/.

[9]cf. https://trufflesuite.com/.

[10]cf. https://infura.io/.

[11]cf. https://javascript.com/.

[12]cf. https://reactjs.org/.

browsers, which are Web 3.0-enabled. All is currently hosted on Amazon Web Services.[13]

Earlier setups with Internet of Things devices as proof type used a Node server[14] to receive the signals from the sensors and forward them to a smart contract, acting as an oracle. The respective code from the github repositories FIN4OracleEngine and FIN4Sensor can be modified to connect other IoT devices.

The Finance 4.0 Development Phases

The FIN4 demonstrator software, called FIN4Xplorer, progressed through several development phases before reaching its current state.

Phase 1: The "Slick but Centralized" (SLIC) Release

Our initial version (developed by Quasi Jouda) performed all blockchain interactions via a server. This architecture offered the convenient, demo-friendly advantage that users could sign up easily (with just a nickname) and participate in creating and claiming tokens within moments of accessing the Web application.

The drawback, however, was that it did not live up to the standards of a distributed project. The use of a centralized server and the custody of users' private keys create vulnerabilities to attacks, while also teaching new users a flawed concept.

We had the responsibility to get it right, since many of our users' first contact with blockchain technology would be through our DApp. Setting up and using a crypto wallet that the users can control was, therefore, important.

Phase 2: The "Fabulous Five" (FAB5) Release

A team of five volunteers (Simon Zachau, Benjamin Degenhart, Kriti Shreshtha, Sangeeta Joseph and Leon Kobinger) completely re-implemented the system to come up with a fully decentralized solution. Their task was to focus on the mechanisms required to link a positive action in the real world to a token balance—i.e., the steps for making claims that are proven in several different ways.

Phase 3: The "Explorer" (XPLR) Release

One member of the "Fabulous Five" (Benjamin Degenhart) continued to work on the system. This phase saw the introduction of more new features including the

---

[13]cf. https://aws.amazon.com/.

[14]cf. https://nodejs.org/.

ability to create user groups, token collections, messages and an own Ether faucet (so users could easily request Ether) and QR codes, as well as transfer token balances. Furthermore, the following four major contributions were integrated.

The first contribution (by Gabriel Hirschbaeck) was a generic smart contract from which different base versions of positive action tokens can be derived in accordance with the taxonomy [21]. Supporting these base versions was a key step towards enabling the breadth of token economies we envision.

The second contribution (by Sergiu Soima) came in the form of the Token Curated Registry (TCR) [22]. A TCR allows an anonymous group of economically incentivized users to maintain a list of entries by submitting votes or challenges. We use this mechanism in our governance layer for maintaining a list of Official Position Action Tokens.

The third contribution (by Piotr Chodyko, Moritz Schindelmann, John Rachwan, and Ling Zhu) redesigned the proving mechanism and created a systematic taxonomy to classify verifiers and implemented an integrated verification system with multiple types of verifiers and decentralized proof of storage [23].

The fourth contribution (by Kriti Shreshtha) was new functionality that allows to incentivize entire communities/collectives rather than just individual users [24].

The Finance 4.0 Demonstrator

As a typical Web3.0 application, FIN4Xplorer[15] consists of two parts: (1) smart contracts on the Ethereum blockchain required for all functionality that should be run in a decentralized, immutable manner and (2) a front end or Decentralized App (DApp) client that serves as a Web interface to the smart contracts. The Ethereum blockchain was chosen as it meets the requirements as an open-source, public blockchain that supports smart contracts. Since it is widely used, one can find much documentation and online resources as well as tap into a large and active developer community.

A user can simply connect to the live version of our demonstrator by visiting https://demo.finfour.net.

From a user perspective, the key difference between a Web 3.0 DApp and a Web 2.0 service is the need for a bridge to the blockchain: a crypto wallet. The first task of a crypto wallet is to connect to the blockchain network, either via a full node run by users themselves or via a gateway service like Infura.[16] Its second task is to appear whenever the user wishes to write data to the blockchain. The recommended crypto wallet to connect to the FIN4 system is MetaMask,[17] which is available both as a browser extension for the desktop (Chrome, Firefox, Opera and Brave) and as a mobile App (iOS and Android). With a crypto wallet, the user can follow the steps to

---

[15] Source code available at https://github.com/FuturICT2/.

[16] cf. https://infura.io/.

[17] cf. https://metamask.io/.

create a new account—or restore an existing account. To connect to FIN4, the user needs to switch from the Main Ethereum Network to the Rinkeby Test Network.[18]

The last step before starting is to acquire free Rinkeby Ether tokens by using either

- the authenticated faucet at faucet.rinkeby.io (in exchange for a public social media post you receive some Ether tokens);
- the FIN4 faucet server available for users on the demo.finfour.net landing page. For this, click the button [Request Ether] and wait for confirmation.

If FIN4 is migrated to the Ethereum main network in the future, real Ether tokens (ETH) will be required for writing transactions to the blockchain. Such tokens cannot be received from faucets for free; they have to be earned through mining or bought at exchanges with cryptocurrency or fiat money.

Information Box: Web 3.0 Technologies Used in Finance 4.0

The smart contracts are written in Solidity[19] and deployed on the Rinkeby testnet[20] via Truffle.[21] Rinkeby is suitable for the development stage as it uses freely available tokens—unlike the Ethereum main net which requires tokens obtained through exchange or mining. We simulate the Ethereum blockchain using Ganache from Truffle.[22] To store media files required by certain proof types, we use IPFS[23] via the Infura gateway.[24] The MetaMask crypto wallet[25] allows users to connect desktop or mobile browsers to the Ethereum network. The frontend is a React app[26] that uses Drizzle from Truffle[27] to connect to the smart contracts on Ethereum.

Learn more about the Web3.0 development tool chain at https://fin4xplorer. readthedocs.io.

After successfully connecting to the FIN4 DApp, the user should see the Home screen (Fig. 13). From there, you can access the Tokens and Claims tab from the navigation bar at the bottom. The three icons in the top right enable users to display a QR code of their token account, refresh the page and show notifications.

---

[18]cf. https://rinkeby.io/.

[19]cf. https://soliditylang.org/.

[20]cf. https://rinkeby.io/.

[21]cf. https://trufflesuite.com/.

[22]cf. https://www.trufflesuite.com/ganache.

[23]cf. https://ipfs.io/.

[24]cf. https://infura.io/.

[25]cf. https://metamask.io/.

[26]cf. https://reactjs.org.

[27]cf. https://trufflesuite.com/drizzle.

Fig. 13 Main screen of the Finance 4.0 DApp (available at https://demo.finfour.net.)

The Tokens tab allows users to create new tokens, as well as view further information about how they work and how to claim them. Viewing a token opens a dedicated page showing details about the design and performance of the token.

The token creator takes the user step by step through the process of creating a new ERC-20[28] token, or "Positive Action Token." Alongside some basic information like a name, a 3 to 5 character long symbol and a description as well as various fundamental properties of the token design have to be specified, which define the economy that can revolve around this token later on. Furthermore, verifiers are added here that define the proofs user have to provide in order to successfully claim this token. None of the choices a token creator makes in this process can be undone —that is why it is important to think carefully about how to design the new token.

The Claims tab follows the same layout as the Tokens tab. Here, you can submit new claims and view a list of previous claims. "Claiming" is the process of saying

---

[28]cf. https://eips.ethereum.org/EIPS/eip-20.

that you did a positive action in the real world and want the respective token for it. If the claim can be automatically verified, the transfer of the respective token happens immediately, otherwise only upon successful delivery of the necessary (manual) proofs that are required from the claiming user.

For governance, the FIN4 system currently offers a Token Curated Registry (TCR) that allows to collectively manage Positive Action Tokens (PAT). When they collected enough reputation (REP), users can claim governance tokens (GOV) for their reputation tokens (REP). Using the same mechanism, users can collectively change the rules of the token registry by voting on parameter changes. Users with enough governance tokens (GOV) can curate the list of Official Positive Action Tokens (OPATs) in the token curated registry.

Other features for communities are token collections and user groups. Token collections are an easy way to access a predefined list of existing tokens. The feature "user groups" allows one to define user groups for managing token collections and for determining participants in social verification mechanisms.

Finally, a basic messaging system allows users to send messages to each other pseudonymously.

The Finance 4.0 Governance System

FIN4 aims to create an open-source, distributed platform for communities willing to incentivize sustainable actions. Sustainability, privacy and individual freedom are key to the platform. FIN4, therefore, incorporates different types of identity and distributed governance on multiple levels.

But how do participants identify themselves? To what extent can reputation replace identity? How can we prevent malicious use and inadequate accumulation of power? And how can we assure participation in governance and meaningful debates?

These questions are far from trivial and can be approached from different perspectives. Certainly, further research is needed before large-scale deployment of the FIN4 system is advised.

Blockchain Governance and Practical Implications

Code—and any implementation of blockchain-based governance—is always embedded in a social context. Every distributed ledger technology (DLT) project is nestled in a political reality, with laws and decision-making procedures, and cannot be seen as fully independent. Whenever we talk about on-(block)chain governance within FIN4, we see the decisions taken as part of a greater social system. And these actions and decisions are bound to the same rules, laws and regulations as other projects.

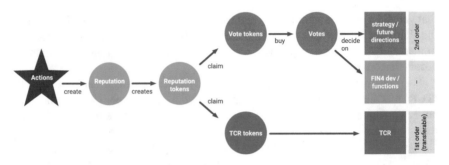

Fig. 14 Potential governance framework for FIN4

Nevertheless, blockchain-based systems allow one to support a power shift from centralized top-down governed structures to federated, self-organizing, bottom-up communities, which do not simply try to cement the status quo.

In the case of FIN4, our goal is to implement a direct democratic voting system linked to the reputation system which is inherent to the platform. Reputation tokens lead to voting rights that can be exercised in all kinds of decisions at different levels—from token curated registries to substantial decisions about the future direction of FIN4.

A number of issues need attention when translating reputation tokens into voting tokens. First, we want reputation to influence voting power. Users with a longer history of honest interactions in the system should enjoy more power. But how much more? To prevent an unbalanced distribution of power and a dictatorship of a group of people, we propose two mechanisms: quadratic voting and a hard cap on reputation tokens. What is more, voting tokens used for voting on system parameters and functions are not returned to users, but instead "burned." This means users would have to carefully consider when to spend voting tokens, since using them means they are gone.

For decisions with a smaller scope, such as voting on which tokens to include in the Token Curated Registry (TCR), one could introduce another type of token—TCR tokens. These could have different qualities compared to the voting tokens above. For example, they may be uncapped and returned to users winning a vote. They could also be transferable.

Voting pools could represent different communities and would help to ensure that the users are not overwhelmed with too many voting options (Fig. 14).

Governance Layer

The governance layer is required to align user incentives towards the creation and maintenance of token economies. It offers mechanisms that allow users to collectively decide on which tokens to include as official FIN4 tokens and which ones to

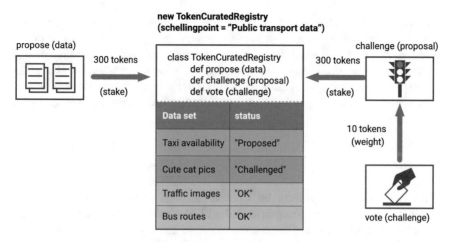

Fig. 15 Staking and voting as basic mechanisms of a Token Curated Registry (based on [25])

reject (first order governance in Fig. 14). On a higher level, the system offers on-chain governance—the possibility for users to collectively change the governance rules (second order governance in Fig. 14).

Any system that permits users to submit new token proposals will sooner or later face the problem of how to deal with spam or malicious tokens. Rather than erecting rules or barriers to restrict token creation, our design utilizes the innovative capacity of independent token proposals. Every token idea is welcome, but adoption as an official FIN4 token requires a sufficiently large share of users to approve the proposal. Based on democratic decision procedures, approvals may also be withdrawn. In any case, the users would collaborate to co-maintain a list of official FIN4 tokens in a Token Curated Registry (TCR) (Fig. 15).

Reputation

The purpose of the reputation tokens (REP) is to help pseudonymous users trust each other in order to interact effectively on the platform. Reputation reflects the positive, platform-sustaining actions performed by a user. These actions can include the active gathering of positive action tokens (zero or low REP reward), participating in proof mechanisms or certain governance mechanisms (medium reward) and successfully proposing official tokens (high reward). In addition, developers should be able to get reputation rewards for contributing to the technical development of the platform.

It should also be possible for users to lose reputation tokens, especially if they interact with the system in a fraudulent way, e.g., by giving false testimony in a social-proof mechanism. However, these mechanisms are still under development.

Tokens based on reputation—as the "qualified money" idea suggests—sometimes raise concerns. However, it is important to realize that money is already judged in this way when we shop online. Factors such as location, type of computer, and other personal qualifiers are used to discriminate among different kinds of online consumers and offer them different prices. Therefore, reputation systems already interfere with our current economic system. FIN4 utilizes reputation not as a mechanism to discriminate against users, but to discourage bad actors and thereby secure a healthy platform. What is more: its opt-in nature and democratic voting give it legitimacy.

Identity

Our idea is to keep the system open, so users can connect different digital identities they have from other providers. Within the FIN4 system, a username linked to an Ethereum address and a reputation score would be already sufficient to establish an identity (ID). But if FIN4 should also allow you to receive tokens tied to a specific citizenship or residency (such as local recycling tokens that may be turned into free museum admission), one could imagine using other forms of IDs to validate claims to certain tokens. It may be beneficial if the system were compatible with both, completely self-sovereign and government-validated digital identity systems.

The ultimate goal of FIN4 is to develop a system design that maximizes privacy (through participation based on self-sovereign digital IDs) and that ensures equality (through caps and quadratic voting), honesty (through reputation) and participation (through easy accessibility).

Proof Mechanisms

Our goal is to create an open-source, distributed platform that allows communities to incentivize sustainable actions using positive action tokens. Users can browse the available FIN4 tokens and see which actions can be carried out in order to earn the respective tokens. After performing the relevant action (planting a tree, collecting litter, or similar), the users need to submit a proof that they actually completed the required action.

But how to prove actions? How can one incentivize users to report actions truthfully? And how can one ensure reliable data is delivered by sensors? This is where proof mechanisms come in.

Token creators on the FIN4 platform will be able to choose from a range of default proof mechanisms for their incentivized actions. These proof mechanisms could include social proofs—requiring *other* platform users to verify user claims—as well as sensor proofs and oracles based on third-party data. Combinations are also possible.

Whenever we need to prove something—in everyday life or within the FIN4 system—there is a trade-off between certainty and usability. With FIN4, proving actions represents a particular challenge. A good balance needs to be found between the effort required and the certainty of proving activities. These proof mechanisms also need to be carefully adapted to each individual token type. For example, a token for promoting a reduction in noise level will use different proofs (including sensors) compared to a token for community cleanup events (removing litter from a public park, for example).

One proof type is the *sensor proof*, which is based on a direct measurement of sustainability data. It requires the least human input and can potentially democratize the provision of and access to data, thereby promoting the value of decentralization while also maximizing efficiency in the proof process. Ideally, data fed into FIN4 should come from these direct measurement sources. Social proofs would only come into play whenever objective measurements are unavailable. Third-party data could be used where data cannot be generated directly within the FIN4 system.

Combinations of proofs will be required to make it more difficult to game the system. Redundancy can be used to increase the reliability of proofs. This is also true in the case of sensors, where a single measurement device may display errors.

With *social proofs*, we generally rely on a testimonial provided by an individual or a sample of typically unrelated people. While users may be able to testify for themselves (auto proof), using a password, signature or similar, we mainly want to work with testimonials provided by peer users. The more users testify to a claim, the more reliable the social proof usually becomes. However, one needs to consider the costs of multiple verifications, which reduce the efficiency of the system. Therefore, social proofs should be straightforward, so random users can do the verification.

Both individual and social proofs can be based on location certain roles or skills, but do not have to. Testimonial power can also be linked to user reputation. But what happens if two validators do not agree? A third validator with a high reputation could be involved to act as a tie breaker. The third validator as well as the one they agree with would receive the regular reputation tokens. Conversely, the user who had submitted false evidence would lose reputation tokens. However, the defeated validator may appeal the decision, putting more reputation tokens at stake. An additional validator would then be called upon to be the judge, with the process continuing in this way if further appeals are submitted.

Honey pots involving fake proof tasks could also be used to catch bad actors and decrease their reputation tokens. These mechanisms may help maintain the integrity of the FIN4 system, while also striking a balance between usability and reliability (see Fig. 16).

Research Outlook: Long-Termism

The first studies and software developments connected with the FIN4 project were initiated by FuturICT 2.0—a FLAG-ERA project supported by the Swiss National Foundation (SNF). FuturICT 2.0 created related concepts, released an initial software demonstrator and spread the idea in academia and beyond (cf. Fig. 17).

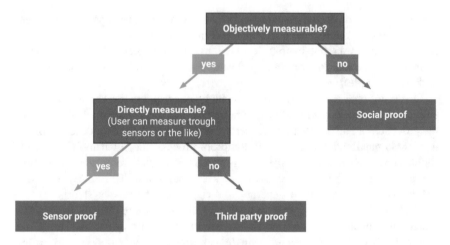

Fig. 16 Type of measurement decides the type of proof mechanisms

FIN4Plus and FIN4Xplorer were two follow-up projects that were supported by EIT Climate-KIC. They initiated a co-design process where the ideas and concepts entered the EIT Climate-KIC strategy for running demonstrations. In that phase, the initial demonstrator software was completely overhauled, improved and extended, thereby incorporating all the different modules into a single, coherent and decentralized demonstrator application ready for small-scale, experimental use.

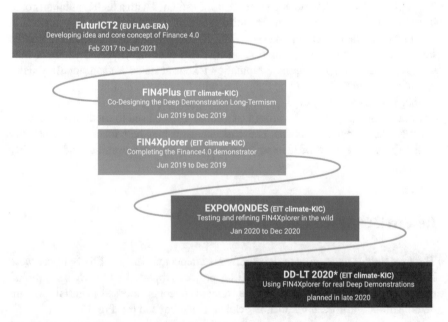

Fig. 17 Finance 4.0 platform evolving across various research projects

We hope to be able to test the FIN4Xplorer application in a series of experiments with real communities, generating feedback from users to help refine the software design and functionality. This would enable a subsequent release based on these insights.

The goal is to be ready to apply the concepts and application to larger-scale experiments, e.g., in the EIT Climate-KIC "Deep Demonstrations on Long-Termism" program.[29]

Systems Innovation. In their strategy document 2019–2022, EIT Climate-KIC argues that innovations at the system level are key to advance the sustainability transformation. Systems innovations refer to "integrated and coordinated interventions in economic, political and social systems and along whole value chains through a portfolio of deliberate and connected innovation experiments" [26]. The proposed approach of using a portfolio of experiments is designed to produce viable pathways towards change by identifying options as well as social and behavioral inflection points and scaling transformative solutions.

Deep Demonstrations. Demonstrating potential for change is central to the transformation needed and for providing inspirational examples of what is possible. These start with a demand-driven approach, working with city authorities, regional bodies, governments and industry leaders, committed to a transformation to net zero emissions and a resilient future. EIT Climate-KIC has initiated eight deep demonstrations to cover a wide range of challenges.

Long-Termism. The design group has co-designed a portfolio of connected experiments that are ready to be planned out and implemented. As part of the design group, we contributed concepts for building incentive systems that promote sustainable action and can serve as basis for sustainability-driven basic income schemes—on the basis of the Finance 4.0 framework.

Over the course of the project, relationships with several organizations and communities have been established to enter the next phase of experimentation:

- The *KISS Foundation*[30] wants to bring their social time-banking scheme online;
- *WWF Romania*[31] aims to prevent poaching with novel incentive systems;
- The *Red Cross* is working on community inclusion currencies;
- *Haus der Materialisierung* (Berlin)[32] promotes circular economy communities;
- *wertfrei*[33] is a platform promoting inclusion and sustainability.

With some organizations, several initial prototypes have been developed during week-long blockchain hackathons for sustainability. Those prototypes can be found online:

- https://github.com/FuturICT2/BETH-2019
- https://github.com/FuturICT2/BIOTS-2018.

---

[29] cf. https://www.climate-kic.org/programmes/deep-demonstrations/.

[30] cf. https://fondation-kiss.ch/.

[31] cf. https://wwf.ro/.

[32] cf. https://hausderstatistik.org/hdm/.

[33] cf. https://wertfreiplattform.ch/.

Summary

The world today faces a range of major sustainability issues: global inequality, financial crises, over-consumption and conflict for natural resources.

By now, there are some common goals with respect to sustainability, as formulated in the United Nation's Sustainable Development Goals and the Paris Agreement. Agreeing on a joint set of goals in a supranational context is certainly important. However, it represents just a first step in a longer transition, because we still face a misalignment of goals and incentive structures.

Therefore, we propose a new approach to achieve sustainability, based on voluntary individual contributions and collective action incentivized by local, real-time feedback (Fig. 18). If we compare the options—a data-driven, AI-controlled society on the one hand and a digitally empowered participatory society on the other hand—the latter is perhaps harder to reach. However, it is expected to be more resilient and more successful in the long run than a top-down controlled society—and more rewarding.

	Top-down Steered Society	Enabled Participatory Society
Decision making	central	distributed
Strategy	big data / machine learning	co-creation / collective intelligence
Operational mode	top-down orders	MOODs
Resource use mitigation	surveillance, citizen score	positive incentivation
Personal freedom	severely limited	maximized

Fig. 18 Two different approaches to the digital society

With the FIN4 system and the associated demonstrator, FuturICT 2.0 has shown that it is technically feasible to introduce a distributed system incentivizing sustainable action. At numerous events and during the first edition of the Climate City Cup,[34] a lot of scientists, companies and individuals around the world have demonstrated their interest in this approach. In subsequent projects that will further extend the FIN4 concept, new partners are expected to join the movement and help establish this novel, participatory approach towards the creation of a more sustainable world and a peaceful, prospering society.

Author Contributions

Mark Ballandies contributed to the sections on Framework and Cryptoeconomics as well as Figs. 5, 7 and 8.

Marcus M. Dapp contributed to the sections on Framework, Crypoeconomics, Technology Landscape, and Research Outlook as well as Figs. 2, 4, 5, 9, 10, 12 and 17.

Benjamin Degenhart contributed to the section on Technology Landscape as well as Fig. 13.

Dirk Helbing developed ideas and strategies for the FuturICT 2.0, Finance 4.0 and Climate City Cup frameworks. He contributed the Abstract and provided various edits and feedbacks.

Stefan Klauser contributed to the Preface of the Finance 4.0 book, the sections on Ambition, Governance System, and to the Summary as well as Figs. 1, 3, 14, 16 and 18.

Anabel-Linda Pardi contributed to the simulation parts mentioned in the Cryptoeconomics section as well as Figs. 10, 11.

Acknowledgements Herewith, we would like to thank everyone who has contributed to the Finance 4.0-related work. The following people, in particular, listed below in alphabetical order, have significantly supported the project at various stages of its concept, design and implementation phases in the past few years: Fatime Ahmeti, Piotr Chodyko, Leonie Flückiger, Thorben Funke, Gabriel Hirschbaeck, Sangeeta Joseph, Qusai Jouda, Leon Kobinger, Anabele-Linda Pardi, Evangelos Pournaras, John Rachwan, Max Rößner, Moritz Schindelmann, Kriti Shreshtha, Alexander Stein, Sergiu Soima, Magnus Wuttke, Simon Zachau, and Ling Zhu.

The authors are also grateful to Dian Balta and his team at TU Munich for the great cooperation in teaching and the joint supervision of student projects.

Lewis Dale and Eoin Jones have provided excellent copy editing support, and Anna-Lena Stach at Relevance House has significantly contributed with her graphical designs and layout of the ebook (technical report), on which this book chapter is based.

Work on the Finance 4.0 system has been financially supported by the Swiss National Science Foundation (Grant No. 170226) as part of the European FLAG ERA project "FuturICT 2.0 – Large scale experiments and simulations for the second generation of FuturICT" (https://futurict2.eu/).

---

[34]cf. https://climatecitycup.org.

In addition, work reported in the research outlook and the demonstrator were supported by EIT Climate-KIC (Grant Nos. 191170, 191354 and 200994) as part of the "Deep Demonstrations on Longtermism" program and the "Thought-Leadership" program (http://www.finfour.net/).

References

1. H. Schandl, M. Fischer-Kowalski, J. West, S. Giljum, M. Dittrich, N. Eisenmenger, A. Geschke, M. Lieber, H. Wieland, A. Schaffartzik, F. Krausmann, S. Gierlinger, K. Hosking, M. Lenzen, H. Tanikawa, A. Miatto, T. Fishman, J. Ind. Ecol. **22**, 827 (2018)
2. M.C. Urban, Science **348**, 571 (2015)
3. UN General Assembly, *Transforming Our World: The 2030 Agenda for Sustainable Development* (Division for Sustainable Development Goals, New York, NY, USA, 2015)
4. Conference of the Parties, *Adoption of the Paris Agreement* [U.N. Doc. FCCC/CP/2015/L.9/Rev.1] (2015) https://documents-dds-ny.un.org/doc/UNDOC/LTD/ G15/283/19/PDF/G1528319.pdf
5. M.C. Ballandies, M.M. Dapp, E. Pournaras, Decrypting distributed ledger design—taxonomy, classification and blockchain community evaluation. Cluster Computing (2021). http://doi.org/ 10.1007/s10586-021-03256-w
6. V. Buterin, *Introduction to Cryptoeconomics* (2017) https://www.youtube.com/watch?v=pKq djaH1dRo. Accessed 23 Dec 2020
7. H.C.A. van Tilborg, S. Jajodia (eds.) *Encyclopedia of Cryptography and Security*, 2nd edn. (Springer, US, 2011)
8. M. Zargham, *Creating Interconnected Collaborative Communities* (2018) https://www.you tube.com/watch?v=nOP6anxiHkk. Accessed 23 Dec 2020
9. M. Dobler, M. Ballandies, V. Holzwarth, On the extension of digital ecosystems for SCM and customs with distributed ledger technologies, in: *2019 IEEE International Conference on Engineering, Technology and Innovation (ICE/ITMC)* (2019). https://doi.org/10.1109/ICE. 2019.8792646
10. K. Wüst, A. Gervais, Do you need a blockchain?, in: *2018 Crypto Valley Conference on Blockchain Technology (CVCBT)* (2018), pp. 45–54
11. R.N. Mantegna, J. Kertész, Focus on statistical physics modeling in economics and finance, New J. Phys. **13**, 025011 (2011)
12. T. Lux, Applications of statistical physics methods in economics: Current state and perspectives, Eur. Phys. J. Spec. Top. **225**, 3255–3259 (2016)
13. A. Sinha, S. Mukherjee, B.K. Chakrabarti, Econophysics through computation, Journal of Physics Through Computation **3**, 1–54 (2020)
14. M.H.R. Stanley, L.A.N. Amaral, S.V. Buldyrev, S. Havlin, H. Leschhorn, P. Maass, M.A. Salinger, H.E. Stanley, Nature **379**, 804 (1996)
15. S.-H. Chen, S.-P. Li, Econophysics: Bridges over a turbulent current, International Review of Financial Analysis **23**, 1–10 (2012)
16. R. Kutner, M. Ausloos, D. Grech, T. Di Matteo, C. Schinckus, H.E. Stanley, Physica A: Statistical Mechanics and Its Applications **516**, 240–253 (2019)
17. D.D. Gatti, S. Desiderio, E. Gaffeo, P. Cirillo, M. Gallegati, *Macroeconomics from the Bottom-Up* (Springer, Mailand, 2011)
18. D. Helbing (ed.), *Social Self-Organization: Agent-Based Simulations and Experiments to Study Emergent Social Behavior* (Springer, Berlin Heidelberg, 2012)
19. F. Abergel, H. Aoyama, B.K. Chakrabarti, A. Chakraborti, A. Ghosh (eds.) *Econophysics of Agent-Based Models* (Springer International Publishing, 2014)
20. C.M. Macal, M.J. North, Agent-based modeling and simulation: ABMS examples, in: *Proc. of the 2008 Winter Simulation Conference* (2008), pp. 101–112

21. G. Hirschbaeck, Software Application to Create General-Purpose Tokens on a Distributed Ledger, Bachelor Thesis, University Foundation San Pablo CEU, 2020. https://doi.org/10.13140/RG.2.2.35923.81447
22. S. Soima, A Blockchain-Based System for Decentralized Curation of Finance 4.0 Tokens, Master Thesis, Technical University Munich (2020). https://doi.org/10.13140/RG.2.2.11484.33921
23. R. John, P. Chodyko, in: *Artificial Intelligence for Cyber Security—Methods, Issues and Possible Horizons or Opportunities*, ed. by S. Misra and A.K. Tyagi. (Springer International Publishing, Cham, 2021)
24. S. Kriti, A Blockchain-Based System to Incentivize Collective Sustainable Behavior in A Community, Master thesis, Technical University Munich (2020)
25. D. de Jonghe, G. Dhameja, T. Debus, G. Pancar, *Curated Governance with Stake Machines.* https://medium.com/@DimitriDeJonghe/curated-governance-with-stake-machines-8ae290 a709b4. Accessed 23 Dec 2020
26. EIT Climate-KIC, *Transformation, in Time* (2019) https://www.climate-kic.org/news/transf ormation-in-time/. Accessed 23 Dec 2020

An Interaction Support Processor to Promote Individual and Systemic Benefits

Dirk Helbing

Abstract *Individual choices, if not sufficiently well coordinated, can lead to bad outcomes, such as systemic instabilities or failures, or "tragedies of the commons." It is, therefore, proposed to use digital assistants to support favorable interactions and avoid undesirable ones. The invention discussed here describes ways to perform these tasks in a decentralized way that also protects sensitive information. Such digital assistants offer better solutions based on local empowerment and coordination rather than on large-scale surveillance and control. In particular, it is suggested to introduce a multi-dimensional value exchange based on multiple new currencies that are linked to reputation values or sensor measurements, which may use the Internet of Things. This novel approach expands the solution space such that new opportunities for favorable interactions arise, which benefits the system and its components. Often, similar results would not be achievable with classical optimization approaches and conventional, one-dimensional value exchange only.*

One day, in late 2012, I decided to write a patent application. It was not for the first time. I had already successfully patented the idea for a self-organized traffic control system together with a colleague.[1]

The new patent application was for an "Interaction Support Processor."[2] It described the concept of digital assistants that would not only lead to better individual decisions, but—above all—they would better coordinate people's decisions

---

This Appendix is a slightly adapted version of the preprint "Interaction Support Processor—and Why the Patenting System Is Broken", available at https://www.researchgate.net/publication/342 040513.

D. Helbing (✉)
ETH Zurich, Computational Social Science, Stampfenbachstrasse 48, 8092 Zurich, Switzerland
e-mail: dhelbing@ethz.ch

[1] D. Helbing and S. Lämmer, Method for coordination of competing processes or for control of the transport of mobile units within a network https://patents.google.com/patent/US8103434B2/en.

[2] Interaction support processor https://patents.google.com/patent/US20160350685A1/en.

so that systemic instabilities and conflicts would be avoided.[3] The invention was about generating individual advantages, but not at the expense of others. Rather, everyone should benefit!

The patent application proposed a "social mirror",[4] which would be a digital representation of how certain decisions would affect the environment and others. My goal was to achieve better decisions through "greater awareness," and to make people want to "behave in a more beautiful way"—quite similar to how a mirror makes them want to "look more beautiful."

The patent application also explained how people could be protected from adverse decisions—by a "social protector". In addition, it described, how they could be made aware of favorable opportunities that they would otherwise overlook, namely, through a further kind of digital assistant: a "social guide". This would also ensure that, as far as possible, "win-lose" situations would be turned into "win-win" situations (by means of compensation payments), so that all parties would benefit from the interaction. For this purpose, the patent application proposed "social money"—new types of money that could, for example, depend on reputation or measurements (see Fig. 1).[5]

The ultimate goal, which should be achieved by the invention, was a world without manipulation, exploitation, and coercion. A world where people and the environment would benefit from digitally assisted, considerate behavior, and from actions that would benefit us all. All this would happen in a way that would use digital technologies for personal empowerment, while protecting our privacy.

The patent, I hoped, would offer a way into a positive digital future, and a way out of the current dystopia. With the patent, I wanted to create opportunities for companies and people, who were engaged for a better future, while there would be obstacles for those, who just cared about profit.

Let me make a bit clearer how the invention would work, so that, in the future, many would benefit, not just a few, as it had been the case in the past. To do this, I will shortly summarize the idea of "social money".

Imagine that we would have measurement methods that measure CO_2, noise, or toxins, or also good things such as resources of various kinds: glass, plastic, metals— or health, knowledge, social, or cultural achievements. Moreover, imagine we do not give them a price in Dollars or Euros, but we measure them in different currencies

---

[3]This idea was somewhat similar to how our traffic assistance systems worked, see e.g. A. Kesting, M. Treiber, M. Schöhof, and D. Helbing (2008) Adaptive cruise control design for active congestion avoidance, Transportation Research C 16(6), 668–683, https://www.sciencedirect.com/science/art icle/pii/S0968090X08000028; S. Lämmer and D. Helbing (2008) Self-control of traffic lights and vehicle flows in urban road networks, J. Stat. Mech., P04019, https://iopscience.iop.org/article/ 10.1088/1742-5468/2008/04/P04019/meta; D. Helbing (2013) Economics 2.0: The natural step towards a self-regulating, participatory market society. Evolutionary and Institutional Economics Review 10, 3–41, https://link.springer.com/article/10.14441/eier.D2013002.

[4]Social mirror: More success through awareness and coordination, https://link.springer.com/cha pter/10.1007/978-3-319-90869-4_17.

[5]Note that the concept of "social money" is somewhat similar to the concept of "qualified money" introduced before.

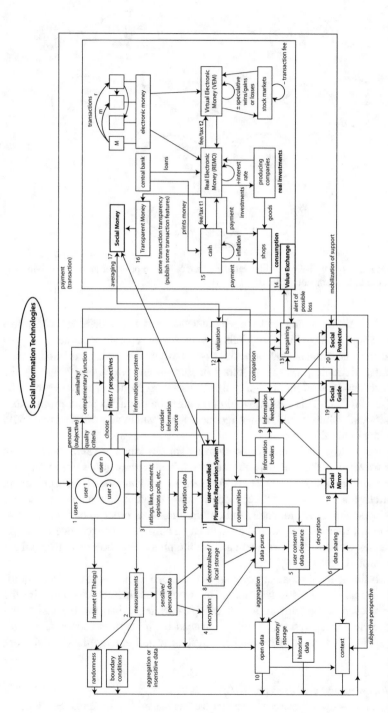

Fig. 1 Illustration of the different parts of the invention

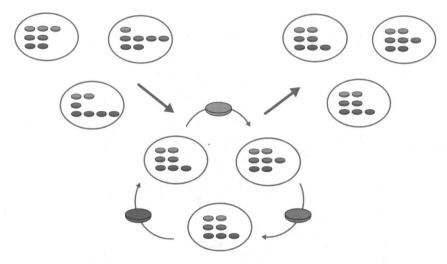

Fig. 2 Illustration of multi-dimensional value exchange, here, a payment process involving and benefitting multiple interaction partners

that cannot be easily exchanged for each other—only at a considerable fee. So, in a sense, we would manage different kinds of values with separate accounts.

Instead of a one-dimensional monetary system, where everything can be converted in an almost frictionless way into Dollars or Euros—and where everything can be bought with one kind of money—a multi-dimensional monetary system would be created (see Fig. 2).[6] This system would no longer be primarily about profit maximization. Social values would matter, too, ecological values as well. And one could also consider cultural values.

Everyone could contribute to the system by various kinds of value creation—in whatever way it suits their talents and interests. When we buy goods or services, we would pay with a mix of currencies to compensate for their social, environmental, and cultural values. So, we would commit not only to profit maximization, but also to achieving social, environmental, and cultural goals, in order to earn the currencies we need. Otherwise, we would have to pay a considerable exchange fee to get the currencies we lack. With an adequate mobile phone app, however, all payment processes would be very easy.

A multi-dimensional monetary system as described above would create a multi-dimensional real-time feedback system. This would be much more suitable for the control—or even self-organization—of complex systems than the basically one-dimensional monetary system of today.[7] Instead of the current economic organization, which wastes a lot of resources, a system would emerge that would work

---

[6]cf. https://www.youtube.com/watch?v=PJGZpV4PUwY.

[7]Qualified Money—A better financial system for the future, https://papers.ssrn.com/sol3/papers.cfm?abstract_id=2526022, published in this book.

similar to nature: a resource-saving circular economy.[8] It would be a new system made possible by a new approach: through multi-dimensional co-evolution rather than one-dimensional optimization: through coordination instead of control. This would create a new kind of economy that would boost a (more) sustainable world and might, thereby, be able to save millions of lives.

With such a multi-dimensional system, the economy could be much better steered in directions that serve the environment and humanity. Several goals could be pursued simultaneously—not just profit maximization. The world would continue to improve through a co-evolutionary process. And we could all participate in it!

Some Background

The invention is focused on interactions among smart system components capable of sensing, information processing, valuation, and information exchange, which could be smart devices such as AI systems, intelligent machines, bots, or robots, or also people using smart devices (i.e., networks of system components, where the components comprise people *and* technology). For example, the interaction support processor could be a particular, novel kind of personal digital assistant. Detailed specifications are made in the main body of the patent.[9]

Sensing (sensor measurements) play(s) a role

- to determine and valuate the local context of the prospective actions and interactions, and of alternative actions and interactions (where possible interventions or possible value exchanges have been added),[10]
- for the measurement of the actions and interactions in the system and their effects (e.g., for a data-driven valuation),
- for a data-driven modeling and simulation of the action and interaction effects,
- for sensor-measurement-based kinds of value exchanges.

Information processing plays a role for data management, for the determination of possible interventions and possible value exchanges, and for the valuation of actions and interactions with and without these.

Valuation is needed to compare a scenario given by prospective actions and interactions with scenarios given by these prospective actions and interactions when possible interventions and possible value exchanges are added to them.

Information exchange is needed to communicate between different system components, particularly in a distributed, privacy-protecting implementation.

---

[8]The FIN4 Project: Towards a Socio-Ecological Finance System, by Dirk Helbing, https://www.youtube.com/watch?v=XnemIMW7e3c.

[9]See [0024]f, [0047], [0117] in https://patents.google.com/patent/US20160350685A1/en.

[10]Throughout the main body of the patent, many ways of determining context by means of modern digital technologies have been described, see https://patentscope.wipo.int/search/en/detail.jsf?docId=WO2015118455.

In contrast to what we have today, we are talking here mainly about a *multi-dimensional value exchange system*.[11] This is important as it increases the optimization space and, therefore, the set of possible solutions, and hence allows for better solutions than without the consideration of this multi-dimensional value exchange system. It creates additional possibilities to improve the system as compared to today's scenario analysis techniques or current monetary compensation schemes in our economy. The proposed multi-dimensionality of value exchange is the main reason why the invention allows to find solutions that benefit all system components—in contrast to the systems known today.

The invention focuses on interventions that consider a *plurality* of value exchanges. This implies that not only feedback effects are being considered, as this is being done by applied "scenario analysis," but that additionally value exchanges are explored. The consideration of *multi-dimensional digitally based value exchanges*[12] is one of the aspects, which sets the invention apart from the state-of-the art in technological, social or economic systems at the time this patent application was submitted.

What the invention proposes is very different from what is being done and discussed today, where each thing, e.g., CO_2, glass bottles for recycling, poisons, or any other kind of externalities is given a certain value or price in Dollars, say, and where there is quite frictionless exchange between different kinds of currencies or assets, which makes today's money-based feedback system effectively one-dimensional (i.e., there is one overall price, which supports utilitarian approaches). In contrast, the system proposed here is designed in such a way that it is a *multi-dimensional* real-time feedback system *in an action space that has been extended by the possibility to exchange multiple kinds of values. Moreover, the invention specifies novel kinds of (monetary) values, which are defined on the basis of measurements or reputation values, for example.*

Further aspects can be illustrated for the case, where a system component's valuation of prospective actions and interactions is done via a goal function G. In classical optimization, a goal function $G(x)$ is optimized as a function of some variables x (where x, accordingly, may represent a vector). As G is a one-dimensional quantity, one can always say whether a solution $G(x_1)$ is better ($>$), worse ($<$), or equal ($=$) in quality. Otherwise (i.e., for a multi-dimensional goal function), the classical method of optimization does not work.

If you have two or more goal functions $G_1, G_2 \ldots$, this kind of $>, <, =$ comparison cannot be done. As one changes x, one goal may be better achieved and the other one may take on a worse value [i.e., $G_1(x_1) > G_1(x)$, while $G_2(x_1) < G_2(x)$]. The invention describes what to do in order to achieve solutions where two or more goal functions are simultaneously improved. Such a solution often does not exist with one kind of value exchange. It requires a multi-dimensional value exchange system.

---

[11] See [0062], [0146]ff, [0156]ff in https://patents.google.com/patent/US20160350685A1/en.
[12] See [0062], [0146]ff, [0156]ff in https://patents.google.com/patent/US20160350685A1/en.

As this content has not been published anywhere else, below I will provide the revised claim set which had finally been submitted for approval in the USA.[13]

Appendix

Claims[14]

1. A computer-implemented method, comprising:
    under the control of one or more computer systems configured with executable instructions,
    maintaining system component data of a plurality of system components in a system component data structure;
    maintaining transaction data of a plurality of transactions in a transaction data structure, wherein a transaction in the plurality of transactions is a record of an interaction between two or more system components of the plurality of system components;
    evaluating components of a prospective transaction among a set of prospective system components, wherein the components include whether each system component of the set of prospective system components has an initial positive valuation of the prospective transaction thereby providing a favorable interaction transaction as to such system components, and which, if any system component of the set of prospective system components has an initial negative valuation of the prospective transaction thereby providing an unfavorable interaction transaction as to such system components;
    determining, based on a computer analysis of the components of the prospective transaction and a rules data structure that defines value exchanges and feedback effects, whether a prospective value exchange or a prospective feedback effect, when added to the prospective transaction, results in an unfavorable interaction transaction as to a particular system

---

[13] There is only this preprint https://www.researchgate.net/publication/342040513, where one can also find the claims I have drafted myself. By the way, my latest claim set starts out with a more technical specification, as it was always intended: A computer-implemented method, comprising a network of system components capable of sensing, information processing, valuation, and information exchange under the control of one or more computer systems configured with executable instructions...

[14] In the meantime, the title of the invention had been changed to "Computer-Based Interactions in Techno-Socio-Economic-Environmental Support Systems with Technical, Social, Economic, and/or Environmental Transaction Management and Processing". Note that it has been stated that these claims would not be patentable in the USA and, hence, the patent application has been abandoned over there. The positive implication of this is that (if I understand patent law correctly) everybody should now be able to use the ideas presented here in the USA and many other countries for free. Note, however, that the application is still pending in some countries.

component being converted into a favorable interaction transaction as to that particular system component;

determining, based on the computer analysis of the components of the prospective transaction and the rules data structure, whether a condition is present in which (1) a proposed value exchange and (2) a proposed feedback effect are present in the rules data structure that, when added to the prospective transaction, results in the prospective transaction being converted into a favorable interaction transaction as to each prospective system component using that prospective transaction; and

outputting, based on whether the condition is present, terms of a modified transaction to each prospective system component, wherein the modified transaction is the prospective transaction modified by the proposed value exchange and the proposed feedback effect.

2. The computer-implemented method of claim 1, wherein the prospective transaction is characterized as to each prospective system component of the prospective transaction as being one of: (1) a win-win situation, (2) a good win-lose situation, (3) a bad win-lose situation, and (4) a lose-lose situation.

3. The computer-implemented method of claim 1, wherein the proposed value exchange or the proposed feedback effect are based on computations done using data provided by a third-party broker.

4. The computer-implemented method of claim 1, wherein the proposed value exchange and the proposed feedback effect further include determining expected behaviors and social norms according to averages of social behaviors over actual measured behaviors.

5–7. (Canceled)

8. A computer-implemented method, comprising:

under the control of one or more computer systems configured with executable instructions,

maintaining system component data of a plurality of system components in a system component data structure;

maintaining transaction data of a plurality of transactions in a transaction data structure, wherein a transaction in the plurality of transactions is a record of an interaction between two or more system components of the plurality of system components;

evaluating components of a prospective transaction among a set of prospective system components, wherein the components include relative valuations of the set of prospective system components participating in the prospective transaction;

aligning value changes of a system and at least one component of the prospective transaction according to a respective valuation of interactions or potential interactions;

determining, based on computer analysis of the components of the prospective transaction and a rules data structure that defines value exchanges and feedback effects, whether a prospective value exchange or a prospective feedback effect, when added to the prospective transaction, results in an unfavorable interaction transaction as to a particular system component being converted into a favorable interaction transaction as to that particular system component; and

flagging the prospective transaction as being one of a favorable transaction, an unfavorable transaction, or a semi-favorable transaction, wherein a semi-favorable transaction is defined as a transaction that is convertible to a favorable transaction via a bargaining and value exchange, wherein an unfavorable transaction is defined as a transaction wherein at least one system component of the set of prospective system components has a negative valuation of the prospective transaction, and a favorable transaction is defined as a transaction wherein each system component of the set of prospective system components has a positive valuation of the prospective transaction.

9.   (Cancelled)

10. The computer-implemented method of claim 8, wherein the prospective transaction comprises sensitive data and the sensitive data is managed by a third-party broker computer system such that it is not available to each of the plurality of system components.

11. The computer-implemented method of claim 8, further comprising determining reputation values and recommendations according to reputation filters, the reputation filters being personally configurable and shared by system components.

12–15. (Cancelled)

16. The computer-implemented method of claim 8, further comprising:
Operating a reputation-based online information filtering system to:

(a) accept a set of ratings, the set of ratings being ratings of online information objects obtained from one or more of the system components;

(b) determine a set of reputation weights, the set of reputation weights being weights of users of the one or more of the system components;

(c) store, into a rating database, data representing the set of ratings and the set of reputation weights;

(d) generate a personal information filter data structure of an information filter derived from the data representing the set of ratings and the set of reputation weights; and

(e) provide viewing user access to the personal information filter data structure, thereby allowing a viewing user to filter online information according to a perspective defined by the set of ratings and the set of reputation weights,

wherein a rating of the set of ratings is a numerical value provided by a rating user for a particular time, weighted by one or more relevance weights and a reputation weight of the rating user and updated over time, rating a specified online information object, *wherein* relevance weights for a posted rating are based on a posting manner in which the posted rating was posted, with a higher relevance weight given to a posting manner that provides greater information about the rating user, *wherein* online information is presentable to the viewing user filtered according to the personal information filter data structure when the viewing user selects to filter according to the personal information filter data structure, and

wherein a set of reputation weights of the rating user are a function of a manner in which the rating user has previously rated other online information objects.

17. The computer-implemented method of claim 16, wherein the information filter is derived from ratings of a plurality of rating system components.

18. The computer-implemented method of claim 16, wherein the personal information filter data structure is in a form sharable among system components, thereby forming socially sharable information filters, the socially sharable information filters being personally configurable by a receiving system component or automatically configurable according to a context.

19. The computer-implemented method of claim 16, further comprising a value exchange system for system components of the value exchange system to use to transfer value, and wherein value transfers to the rating user are, at least in part, a function of a reputation weight of that rating user.

20. The computer-implemented method of claim 16, further comprising a feedback system, wherein the reputation weight of the rating user varies according to an alignment of the rating user with a set of social media expectations.

21. The computer-implemented method of claim 16, wherein the one or more relevance weights comprise one or more of:

   (a) a time span between a rating time when the rating user rated a particular online information object and when that rating is used in a filter,
   (b) the posting manner in which the rating user posted the rating, the posting manner being one of anonymously, pseudo-anonymously, or personalized,
   (c) a frequency with which the rating user posts ratings,
   (d) a number of ratings the rating user posted, and
   (e) a quality with which the rating user classified the particular online information object.

22. The reputation-based online information filtering system of claim 21, wherein a first rating posted anonymously is given a first relevance weight, a second rating posted pseudo-anonymously is given a second relevance weight, and a personalized rating identifying the rating user is given a third relevance weight, wherein the first relevance weight is lower than the

second relevance weight, and the second relevance weight is lower than the third relevance weight.

23. The reputation-based online information filtering system of claim 21, wherein the quality is a function of whether a class, selected from among advertisement, opinion, or fact, into which the rating user classified the particular online information object is a class consistent with a class selected by other system components for the particular online information object.

24. The reputation-based online information filtering system of claim 21, further comprising a filter interaction system, wherein personal information filter data structures are exchanged among system components of the filter interaction system, at least one exchange of which includes a corresponding transfer of value between system components.

25. The reputation-based online information filtering system of claim 16, wherein the rating, by the rating user, of a particular online information object, is weighted by a number of ratings previously made by the rating user, wherein the rating is down-weighted when the number of ratings previously made by the rating user is high or frequent, and wherein the rating is up-weighted when the number of ratings previously made by the rating user is low or infrequent.

26. The reputation-based online information filtering system of claim 16, wherein a rating of the specified online information object over a plurality of rating users is determined according to an equation:

$$r_j(t) = \frac{\sum_i r_{ij}(t_{ij}) f_{ij}(t_{ij}) w_i(t_{ij}) p^{t-t_{ij}}}{\sum_i f_{ij}(t_{ij}) w_i(t_{ij}) p^{t-t_{ij}}} = \langle r_{ij} \rangle_i$$

wherein $r_j(t)$ is the rating of an online information object, j, at time t, i is an index of the rating user, $r_{ij}(t)$ is the rating of the online information object, j, given by rating user i, $w_i(t)$ is the rating given at time t, p is a decay factor ranging from 0 to 1, and f is a reliability factor,

wherein the rating of the online information object, j, over the plurality of rating users is further weighed by a variance of ratings over the plurality of rating users, and

wherein the rating, $r_j(t) = N_j(t)/D_j(t)$, of the online information object, j, over the plurality of rating users is stored in computer memory as a nominator, $N_j(t) = N_j(t')p^{t-t'} + r_{ij}(t)f_{ij}(t)w_i(t)$, and a denominator, $D_j(t) = D_j(t')p^{t-t'} + f_{ij}(t)w_i(t)$, and a previous updating time, t'.

27. The reputation-based online information filtering system of claim 16, wherein the specified online information object is one or more of an item of content or posting relating to a product, company, or subject.

28. A computer-implemented method, comprising:
instantiating a plurality of system components, implemented using one or more computer systems configured with executable instructions, wherein one or more of the plurality of system components is configured to

perform sensing, information processing, valuation computation, and/or information exchange;

maintaining a system component data structure, wherein a system component data structure comprises data about a system component;

maintaining an action data structure comprising a plurality of action data records, wherein an action data record comprises data about an action of a system component of the plurality of system components;

maintaining an interaction data structure comprising interaction records, wherein an interaction record is a record of an interaction between two or more system components of the plurality of system components;

determining, for each given system component in the plurality of system components, a valuation of prospective actions and prospective interactions between the given system component and other system components;

determining possible feedback effects;

determining a plurality of possible value exchanges;

determining for the given system components in the plurality of system components, valuations of the prospective actions and the prospective interactions between the given system component and other system components when the possible feedback effects or possible value exchanges are added to the prospective actions and prospective interactions, based at least upon a data analysis of previous interactions or a computer simulation; and

identifying, based on computer analyses, whether a condition exists in which proposed interventions result in the prospective interactions being converted into favorable interactions with improved valuations.

29. The computer-implemented method of claim 28, wherein the proposed interventions are used to prevent negative valuations.

30. The computer-implemented method of claim 28, wherein the possible value exchanges or the possible feedback effects are based on distributed computations such that other system components are excluded from access to sensitive data.

31. The computer-implemented method of claim 28, wherein the possible value exchanges and the possible feedback effects further consider expected behaviors of system components based on averages of actually measured behaviors or desired behaviors based on stated preferences or maximum possible values of certain goal functions.

32. The computer-implemented method of claim 28, wherein a multi-dimensional feedback system and value exchange system is implemented to support self-organization of a system comprising a plurality of interacting system components.

33. The computer-implemented method of claim 28, wherein the valuations of the prospective actions and the prospective interactions take into account a reputation value of a plurality of reputation values related to system components, actions, or interactions.

34. The computer-implemented method of claim 33, wherein the reputation value is determined by sensor measurements.

35. The computer-implemented method of claim 33, wherein the reputation value is determined by reputation filters.

36. The computer-implemented method of claim 33, wherein the reputation value is used to define values in a value exchange system.

37. The computer-implemented method of claim 33, wherein the reputation value is determined by ratings.

38. The computer-implemented method of claim 37, wherein ratings of different system components are scaled in such a way that each considered system component has a same overall weight when rating system components, actions, or interactions, independently of a number of ratings sent.

39. The computer-implemented method of claim 37, wherein a rating of a specified online information object over a plurality of rating system components is determined according to an equation:

$$r_j(t) = \frac{\sum_i r_{ij}(t_{ij}) f_{ij}(t_{ij}) w_i(t_{ij}) p^{t-t_{ij}}}{\sum_i f_{ij}(t_{ij}) w_i(t_{ij}) p^{t-t_{ij}}} = \langle r_{ij} \rangle_i$$

wherein $r_j(t)$ is the rating of an online information object, j, at time t, i is an index of the rating system component, $r_{ij}(t)$ is the rating of the online information object, j, given by rating system component i, $w_i(t)$ is the rating given at time t, p is a decay factor ranging from 0 to 1, and f is a reliability factor,

wherein the rating of the online information object, j, over the plurality of rating system components is further weighed by a variance of ratings over the plurality of rating system components, and

wherein the rating, $r_j(t) = N_j(t)/D_j(t)$, of the online information object, j, over the plurality of rating system components is stored in computer memory as a nominator, $N_j(t) = N_j(t')p^{t-t'} + r_{ij}(t)f_{ij}(t)w_i(t)$, and a denominator, $D_j(t) = D_j(t')p^{t-t'} + f_{ij}(t)w_i(t)$, and a previous updating time, t'.

40. A computer-implemented method, comprising:

instantiating a plurality of system components, implemented using one or more computer systems configured with executable instructions, wherein one or more of the plurality of system components is configured to perform sensing, information processing, valuation computation, and/or information exchange;

maintaining a system component data structure, wherein a system component data structure comprises data about a system component;

maintaining an action data structure comprising a plurality of action data records, wherein an action data record comprises data about an action of a system component of the plurality of system components;

maintaining an interaction data structure comprising interaction records, wherein an interaction record is a record of an interaction between two or more system components of the plurality of system components;

evaluating components of a prospective interaction among a set of considered system components, wherein considered system components include references to relative valuations of a set of prospective system components of the prospective interaction;

aligning value changes of a system and at least one component of the prospective interaction according to a respective valuation of interactions or potential interactions;

determining, based on computer analysis of the prospective interaction and a rules data structure that defines value exchanges and feedback effects, whether a prospective value exchange or a prospective feedback effect, when added to the prospective interaction, results in an unfavorable interaction as to a particular system component being converted into a favorable interaction as to that particular system component; and

flagging the prospective interaction as being a favorable interaction, an unfavorable interaction, or a semi-favorable interaction, wherein a semi-favorable interaction is defined as an interaction that is convertible into a favorable interaction via a value exchange, wherein an unfavorable interaction is defined as an interaction wherein at least one system component of the set of prospective system components has a negative valuation of the prospective interaction, and a favorable interaction is defined as an interaction wherein each system component of the set of prospective system components has a positive valuation of the prospective interaction.

41.   The computer-implemented method of claim 40, wherein the prospective interaction comprises exchange of sensitive data and the sensitive data is managed in a distributed way by third-party computer systems such that excluded from access by other system components.

42.   The computer-implemented method of claim 40, considering a reputation value of a plurality of reputation values related to system components, actions, or interactions.

43.   The computer-implemented method of claim 42, wherein the reputation value is determined by sensor measurements.

44.   The computer-implemented method of claim 42, wherein the reputation value is determined by reputation filters.

45.   The computer-implemented method of claim 42, wherein the reputation value is used to define values in a value exchange system.

46.   The computer-implemented method of claim 42, wherein the reputation value is determined by ratings.

47.   The computer-implemented method of claim 46, wherein ratings of different system components are scaled in such a way that every considered system component has the same overall weight when rating system components, actions, or interactions, independently of a number of ratings sent.

48.   The computer-implemented method of claim 46, wherein a rating of a specified online information object over a plurality of rating system components is determined according to an equation:

$$r_j(t) = \frac{\sum_i r_{ij}(t_{ij}) f_{ij}(t_{ij}) w_i(t_{ij}) p^{t-t_{ij}}}{\sum_i f_{ij}(t_{ij}) w_i(t_{ij}) p^{t-t_{ij}}} = \langle r_{ij} \rangle_i$$

wherein $r_j(t)$ is the rating of an online information object, j, at time t, i is an index of the rating system component, $r_{ij}(t)$ is the rating of the online information object, j, given by rating system component i, $w_i(t)$ is the rating given at time t, p is a decay factor ranging from 0 to 1, and f is a reliability factor,

wherein the rating of the online information object, j, over the plurality of rating system components is further weighed by a variance of ratings over the plurality of rating system components, and

wherein the rating, $r_j(t) = N_j(t)/D_j(t)$, of the online information object, j, over the plurality of rating system components is stored in computer memory as a nominator, $N_j(t) = N_j(t')p^{t-t'} + r_{ij}(t)f_{ij}(t)w_i(t)$, and a denominator, $D_j(t) = D_j(t')p^{t-t'} + f_{ij}(t)w_i(t)$, and a previous updating time, t'.

49. A computer-implemented method for promoting participatory value or information exchange, comprising:

under the control of one or more computer systems configured with executable instructions,

promoting responsible exchange by at least partial transparency of transactions;

representing a plurality of money categories; and

introducing at least one transaction charge for converting among the plurality of money categories.

50. The computer-implemented method of claim 49, wherein the at least one transaction charge is an exchange fee and/or a tax.

51. The computer-implemented method of claim 49, further comprising distinguishing among money of the plurality of money categories in order to encourage particular kinds of consumption or real investments or other desired effects, actions, or interactions.

52. The computer-implemented method of claim 49, wherein the plurality of money categories comprises cash, real electronic money, virtual electronic money, and/or multi-dimensional money.

53. The computer-implemented method of claim 49, wherein the prospective interaction comprises exchange of sensitive data and the sensitive data is managed in a distributed way by third-party computer systems such that excluded from access by other system components.

54. The computer-implemented method of claim 49, considering a reputation value of a plurality of reputation values related to system components, actions, or interactions.

55. The computer-implemented method of claim 54, wherein the reputation value is determined by sensor measurements.

56. The computer-implemented method of claim 54, wherein the reputation value is determined by reputation filters.

57.   The computer-implemented method of claim 54, wherein the reputation value is used to define values in a value exchange system.

58.   The computer-implemented method of claim 54, wherein the reputation value is determined by ratings.

59.   The computer-implemented method of claim 58, wherein ratings of different system components are scaled in such a way that every considered system component has the same overall weight when rating system components, actions, or interactions, independently of number of ratings sent.

60.   The computer-implemented method of claim 58, wherein a rating of a specified online information object over a plurality of rating system components is determined according to an equation:

$$r_j(t) = \frac{\sum_i r_{ij}(t_{ij}) f_{ij}(t_{ij}) w_i(t_{ij}) p^{t-t_{ij}}}{\sum_i f_{ij}(t_{ij}) w_i(t_{ij}) p^{t-t_{ij}}} = \langle r_{ij} \rangle_i$$

wherein $r_j(t)$ is the rating of an online information object, j, at time t, i is an index of the rating system component, $r_{ij}(t)$ is the rating of the online information object, j, given by rating system component i, $w_i(t)$ is the rating given at time t, p is a decay factor ranging from 0 to 1, and f is a reliability factor,

wherein the rating of the online information object, j, over the plurality of rating system components is further weighed by a variance of ratings over the plurality of rating system components, and

wherein the rating, $r_j(t) = N_j(t)/D_j(t)$, of the online information object, j, over the plurality of rating system components is stored in computer memory as a nominator, $N_j(t) = N_j(t')p^{t-t'} + r_{ij}(t) f_{ij}(t) w_i(t)$, and a denominator, $D_j(t) = D_j(t')p^{t-t'} + f_{ij}(t) w_i(t)$, and a previous updating time, t'.

Glossary

Blockchain A blockchain is a distributed ledger that is collectively written and maintained by a network through a distributed consensus mechanism.

Cognitive dissonance The mental conflict that arises when ingrained beliefs or assumptions are contradicted by new information.

Consensus Consensus is the mechanism through which entries are written to the distributed ledger technologywhile adhering to a set of rules that all participants enforce when an entry containing transactions is validated.

Cryptocurrency A cryptocurrency is a digital asset designed to work as a medium of exchange using cryptography to secure the transactions and to control the creation of addition units of the currency. (Wikipedia—cited in Technical Report M12 where the definition is somewhat longer).

Cryptoeconomic Design (CED) The options and choices of how a cryptoeconomy regulates value exchange among its participants is referred to as cryptoeconomic design (CED). CED plays a key role in the stability of a DLT system in terms of convergenceliveness, and fairness.

Crypto wallet A cryptocurrency wallet is a physical devicea desktop, or mobile app, which stores public and/or private keys to control cryptocurrencies. They often also offer the functionality of encrypting and/or signing information (e.g., to execute a smart contract or cryptocurrency transaction. Example: MetaMask is a mobile app to manage the Ethereum cryptocurrency

DApp A decentralized application within the context of Web 3.0 which does not rely on a centralized provider.

Distributed Ledger Technology (DLT) Distributed ledger technology encompasses systems of distributed ledgersconsensus mechanisms, and other elements. Here, nodes participate in a distributed data structure which contains entries serving as digital records of actions, governed by a consensus mechanism. A blockchain is a type of DLT.

Externality An externality is a cost or benefit that affects a party who did not choose to incur that cost or benefit.

M. M. Dapp et al. (eds.), *Finance 4.0—Towards a Socio-Ecological Finance System*, SpringerBriefs in Applied Sciences and Technology, https://doi.org/10.1007/978-3-030-71400-0

Fiat money Conventional paper- and coin-based currency issued by a centralized entitytypically a central bank, and declared as legal tender by governments. Examples include euros, dollars, and pounds sterling.

Fork In blockchain terminologya fork typically refers to a situation in which a previously incompatible change in protocol occurs, resulting in the divergence of two sets of protocol. For instance, this can happen when a community around a cryptocurrency disagrees on the implementation of code changes, thereby splitting the community and creating a new token in parallel with the existing token following the established rule set.

Gas In the Ethereum protocolgas is the fee required in order to carry out a transaction or run a smart contract on the blockchain.

ICT Abbreviation for Information and Communication Technology.

Internet of Things (IoT) The Internet of Things is a system of interrelated devices-machines, objects, animals or people that are assigned unique identifiers and given the ability to transfer data over a network without the need for manual interaction.

Meta tokens Meta tokens are tokens that give a user access to platform services and/or the right to participate in decisions that concern the overall structureimplementation, and further development of a system.

Oracle Blockchains cannot directly communicate with the outside world. They therefore rely on trustworthy external data sourcesknown as oracles. Oracles can be based on software (websites and portals) or hardware (IoT sensors).

Proof of Stake A proof-of-stake protocol is a consensus mechanism according to which network participants can mine or validate entries depending on the number of tokens they hold.

Proof of Work A proof-of-work protocol is a consensus mechanism that secures the network by requiring work from participants in order to write to the blockchain. In the case of Bitcoinfor exampleminers have to expend processing power and energy in order to solve hash functions and mine a new block.

Quadratic voting Quadratic voting is a means of decision making that helps prevent problems associated with the accumulation of power in multi-vote systems. The "price" of a vote equals its square each additional therefore comes at a significantly higher price.

Smart contract A piece of executable software code that is written onto the Ethereum blockchain. Once deployedit is immutable and can be executed by anyone on the network.

Token A token is a store of value issued within a DLT system and which can be used as a medium of exchange or unit of account.

Token curated registry (TCR) A list of objects (e.g. web linkstokens, etc.) that are maintained by a group of users. They manage the list through proposing, challenging, and voting using a special TCR token. In the case of Finance 4.0, the GOV token is used to manage the list of official Positive Action Tokens.

Transaction Transactions are the digital representations of actions that are logged in the distributed ledger of a DLT system.

Web 2.0 The Internet of online applications that are offered by central providers. The most well-known examples of these providers include Facebook, Amazon, and Google.

Web 3.0 The emerging form of decentralized online applications which do away with the need for central providers.

Printed in the United States
by Baker & Taylor Publisher Services